Exercises

1. *Example:*
your / Pam
— What's your name?
— My name's Pam.

1. his / Dave
2. her / Rosie
3. your / Charlie

2. *Example:*
your motorbike
Where's your motorbike?

1. your sister
2. Pam
3. our house
4. his motorbike
5. my brother

3. *Example:*
she / our garden
Look! She's in our garden.

1. he / your house
2. your motorbike / my house
3. Pam / your garden
4. your brother / our garden
5. her sister / our garden

4. *Example:*
7 o'clock
It's seven o'clock.

1. 6 o'clock It is six o'clock
2. 1 o'clock It is one "
3. 10 o'clock It is ten o'clock
4. 3 o'clock It is three "
5. 9 o'clock It is nine "
6. 12 o'clock It is twelve
7. 2 o'clock
8. 8 o'clock
9. 4 o'clock
10. 5 o'clock

Summary of grammar

The verb « to be » (singular)

I'm Pam Carter.
You're Charlie Kipper.
He's Dave Carter.
She's Rosie Carter.
It's our garden.

Contractions

I'm	I am
You're	You are
He's	He is
She's	She is
It's	It is
name's	name is
Who's	Who is

1

Notes de grammaire

1. **I'm Pam Carter.**
   He's Dave Carter.

En anglais, surtout dans le langage parlé, vous trouverez fréquemment des formes contractées (« contractions »). Ici donc, on dit « I'm » et « He's » (formes contractées) et non « I am » et « He is » (formes complètes).

2. **My brother.** Mon frère.
   My sister. Ma sœur.
   He's in his house. Il est dans sa maison.
   She's in her garden. Elle est dans son jardin.

Les noms communs anglais n'ont pas de genre comme en français. A l'inverse du français, l'adjectif possessif s'accorde avec le possesseur.

3. **Pam's fine. She's fine.**
   Dave's fine. He's fine.
   My motorbike's fine. It's fine.

En anglais, on emploie « he » et « she » lorsqu'il s'agit de personnes, « it » lorsqu'il s'agit de choses.

4. **To be.** Être.

L'infinitif se forme avec « to » devant le verbe.

Vocabulaire

brother frère
door porte
garden jardin
house maison
motorbike motocyclette
name nom
sister sœur

my mon, ma, mes
your ton, ta, tes (votre, vos)
her son, sa, ses
his son, sa, ses
our notre, nos

in dans

and et

now maintenant

Where? Où?
Who? Qui?

Hello! Bonjour!
How are you? Comment vas-tu? Comment allez-vous?
I'm very sorry. Je suis désolé.
I'm very well. Je vais très bien.
It's fine. C'est bien.
Look! Regarde! Regardez!
Oh dear! Oh la la!
Thank you! Merci!
This is ... Voici ... (quand on présente quelqu'un)
Yes. Oui.

Quatrième page

What time is it? Quelle heure est-il?
It's one o'clock. Il est une heure.

2

Exercises

1. *Example:*
your sister
— How's your sister?
— She's fine, thank you.

1. Pam
2. your brother
3. your motorbike
4. you
5. you and Rosie
6. your parents

2. *Example:*
they / in Brighton
— Are they in Brighton?
— Yes, they are.

1. he / on holiday
2. we / at school
3. they / at home
4. she / in Italy
5. he / in London
6. Pam and Dave / in England

3. *Example:*
Paris / in England
— Is Paris in England?
— No, it isn't.

1. Charlie / at home
2. dinner / ready
3. Mr and Mrs Carter / here
4. London / in France
5. we / in Rome
6. you / in England

4. *Example:*
she / in London
— Why's she in London?
— Because she's on holiday.

1. he / in England
2. Mr and Mrs Carter / in Italy
3. your brother / in Spain
4. you / in Brighton
5. his sister / in Germany
6. she / in Rome

Summary of grammar

The verb « to be » (plural)

We're You're They're	in Italy.

Short answers

Am I Are you Is he, she, it Are we Are you Are they	in Italy?	Yes,	I am. you are. he, she, it is. we are. you are. they are.	No,	I'm not. you aren't. he, she, it isn't. we aren't. you aren't. they aren't.

Contractions

We are	We're
They are	They're
He is not	He isn't
They are not	They aren't

2

Notes de grammaire

1. **She isn't here.**
   They aren't here.

Notez ces deux formes contractées du verbe « to be » à la forme négative : « She isn't » (She is not) et « They aren't » (They are not).

Is she at home? Yes, she is.
Is she in Italy? No, she isn't.

Dans une « short answer » affirmative on n'emploie pas la forme contractée.

2. **Are you on holiday, Pam?** Es-tu en vacances, Pam?
   Are you on holiday, Dave and Rosie? Êtes-vous en vacances, Dave et Rosie?

« You » correspond à « tu » et à « vous », singulier et pluriel.

3. **Our garden.** Notre jardin.
   Our parents. Nos parents.

L'adjectif possessif est invariable.

4. **Notez l'absence de l'article défini dans les expressions « at home, at school ».**

Vocabulaire

dinner dîner
England Angleterre
Italy Italie
mother mère
Mr Carter Monsieur Carter
Mrs Carter Madame Carter
wife femme (épouse)

this ceci

good bon
nice agréable / aimable / gentil
quiet tranquille
ready prêt

here ici

too aussi

because parce que
but mais
or ou

Why? Pourquoi?

to have dinner dîner

at home à la maison
at school à l'école
Come in! Entre! / Entrez!
Here's Charlie. Voici Charlie.
It's hot and sunny. Il fait chaud et il y a du soleil.
No. Non.
on holiday en vacances
Taste this! Goûte / Goûtez ceci!

Ask and answer questions about ... Posez des questions sur ... et répondez.
Ask and answer more questions ... Posez davantage de questions et répondez.

3

Exercises

1. *Example:*
this / camera
— What's this?
— It's a camera.

1. that / motorbike
2. those / parcels
3. this / umbrella
4. these / pens
5. that / picture
6. those / bones

2. *Example:*
that / umbrella (Yes)
— Is that your umbrella?
— Yes, it is.

1. this / dog (Yes)
2. these / books (No)
3. that / brother (Yes)
4. this / shop (No)
5. those / sisters (Yes)
6. this / camera (No)

3. *Example:*
3.05
It's five past three.

1. 2.45
2. 5.25
3. 9.50
4. 11.30
5. 8.40
6. 1.55
7. 4.10
8. 6.15
9. 10.35
10. 7.55
11. 8.20
12. 12.15

4. Contractions
Example:
It is for you.
It's for you.

1. It is very quiet here.
2. Where is my motorbike?
3. I am at school.
4. They are in Italy.
5. She is on holiday.
6. They are not my books.
7. Our parents are not here.
8. How is Mr Carter?
9. It is not for Rosie. It is for Pam.
10. Hey, I am not ready!
11. Who is that?
12. Charlie is not at home.

Summary of grammar

Demonstrative pronouns

What	**is**	**this?** **that?**
	are	**these ?** **those ?**

Indefinite article

It's	**a car.** **an umbrella.**
They're	**cars.** **umbrellas.**

3

Notes de grammaire

1. **What's this? What are these?**
   What's that? What are those? } Qu'est-ce que c'est?

On emploie « this » (pluriel — « these ») pour désigner les objets proches, et « that » (pluriel — « those ») pour des objets plus éloignés.

2. **A car.** Une voiture.
   A camera. Un appareil photo.
   An umbrella. Un parapluie.

L'article indéfini n'est ni masculin ni féminin, mais il a deux formes.
On emploie « a » devant une consonne, et « an » devant une voyelle.

   It's a cup. C'est une tasse.
   They're cups. Ce sont des tasses.

L'article indéfini n'existe pas au pluriel.

3. **La plupart des noms forment leur pluriel en ajoutant un « s » au singulier (ou « es » si le nom se termine par « s, sh, ch, x »).**

Le pluriel se prononce [s] après « p, t, k, f » (cups, motorbikes, lights), [z] après « b, d, g, v, l, m, n, r » (friends, names, pens) et [iz] après « ss, sh, ch, x, se, ge » (classes, pages, sixes).

Vocabulaire

bag sac
bone os
book livre
camera appareil photo
chair chaise
classroom salle de classe
cup tasse
dog chien
friend ami(e)
light lumière
morning matin
parcel paquet
pen stylo
picture dessin / tableau
shop magasin
thing chose
umbrella parapluie
uncle oncle
window fenêtre

a un, une
an un, une
for pour
from de / de la part de

really vraiment

to look at regarder

Happy birthday! Joyeux anniversaire!
Thank you very much. Merci beaucoup.

Quatrième page

Excuse me! Excuse-moi / Excusez-moi!
Please. S'il te plaît / S'il vous plaît.

It's five to three. Il est trois heures moins cinq.
It's ten past three. Il est trois heures dix.
It's quarter past three. Il est trois heures et quart.
It's half past three. Il est trois heures et demie.

Exercises

1. *Example:*
that (Charlie / hat)
— What's that?
— It's Charlie's hat.

1. this (Rosie / record)
2. these (Dave / socks)
3. that (Mr and Mrs Carter / house)
4. those (Pam / shoes)
5. this (Uncle Bob / pipe)
6. these (Arthur / bones)

2. *Example:*
apple / that (Rosie)
— Whose apple is that?
— It's Rosie's apple.

1. umbrella / this (Mrs Carter)
2. garage / that (Charlie)
3. pens / these (Rosie)
4. books / those (Dave)
5. chair / this (Pam)
6. motorbike / that (Charlie)

3. *Example:*
Rosie's socks (Yes)
— Are those Rosie's socks?
— Yes, they're her socks.

1. Uncle Bob's hat (No)
2. Mr and Mrs Carter's car (Yes)
3. Rosie's socks (No)
4. your bag (No)
5. Dave's cup (Yes)
6. my book (Yes)

4. *Example:*
your job / doctor
— What's your job?
— I'm a doctor.

1. his job / farmer
2. their jobs / politicians
3. her job / teacher
4. our jobs / receptionists
5. your job / mechanic
6. his job / vet
7. her job / secretary
8. their jobs / doctors

Summary of grammar

Possessives

Whose	**hat is it?** **hats are they?**

It's	**my** **your** **his** **her** **our** **your** **their**	**hat.**
They're		**hats.**

It's	**Pam's** **Dave's** **Mr Carter's**	**hat.**
They're		**hats.**

4

Notes de grammaire

1. **Whose hat is this?** A qui est ce chapeau?
   It's Charlie's hat. C'est le chapeau de Charlie.

Le cas possessif se forme en ajoutant « 's » au possesseur.
N. B. Ne confondez pas la forme contractée de « is » ('s) et le « 's » du cas possessif.

2. **He's a mechanic.** Il est mécanicien.
   They're doctors. Ils sont médecins.

L'emploi de l'article indéfini est obligatoire au singulier devant les noms de métiers.

Vocabulaire

apple pomme
car voiture
Dad papa
desk bureau / pupitre
hat chapeau
junk collector brocanteur
mechanic mécanicien
Mum maman
record disque
shoe chaussure
sock chaussette
street rue

their leur, leurs

again de nouveau / encore une fois

to à

to go aller

Quatrième page

doctor médecin
farmer fermier
job métier
policeman policier
politician homme politique
receptionist réceptionniste
secretary secrétaire / dactylo
teacher professeur
vet vétérinaire

Exercises

1. *Example:*
cinema
Excuse me, where's the cinema, please?

1. supermarket
2. shops
3. beach
4. Park Street
5. car park
6. gardens

2. *Example:*
Rosie / school (No)
— Is Rosie at school?
— No, she isn't.

1. Arthur / garden (Yes)
2. Mike and Jenny / supermarket (No)
3. Uncle Bob / shop (Yes)
4. your books / table (No)
5. Mrs Carter / home (Yes)
6. keys / floor (No)

3. *Example:*
tickets / on / chair / floor
The tickets aren't on the chair. They're on the floor.

1. cinema / behind / supermarket / garage
2. keys / in / basket / bag
3. Miko and Jenny / in front of / shop / school
4. records / under / books / shopping
5. umbrella / in / house / garden
6. light switch / near / door / window

4. *Example:*
your hat / green
— What colour's your hat?
— It's green.

1. Uncle Bob's pipe / brown
2. Mr and Mrs Carter's car / blue
3. Charlie's hat / red
4. Mr Carter's socks / yellow and pink
5. Miss Smart's bikini / yellow
6. Dave's shoes / brown

Summary of grammar

Definite article

Where	**is**	**the key?**
	are	**the keys?**

It's **They're**	**on**	**the desk.** **the floor.** **the chair.**

5

Notes de grammaire

1. **The car.** La voiture.
   The basket. Le panier.
   The keys. Les clés.

En anglais, l'article défini est invariable.

2. **Miss Smart's green.** Mademoiselle Smart est verte.
   Her bikini's black. Son bikini est noir.
   They're dirty. Ils / elles sont sales.

En anglais, les adjectifs qualificatifs sont invariables.

Vocabulaire

basket panier
car park parking
finger doigt
flat appartement
floor plancher
foot pied
key clef
keyhole trou de serrure
light switch interrupteur
pocket poche
sentence phrase
shopping les courses
supermarket supermarché
ticket billet / ticket

late en retard

like comme

behind derrière
in front of devant
near près (de)
on sur
under sous
over there là-bas

Be quiet! Tais-toi / Taisez-vous!
Here it is! Le voici!
Hurry up! Dépêche-toi / Dépêchez-vous!

Quatrième page

Miss Smart Mademoiselle Smart
beach plage
bikini bikini (maillot deux-pièces)
colour couleur

black noir
blue bleu
brown brun (bronzé)
dirty sale
green vert
pink rose
red rouge
white blanc
yellow jaune

It's cold. Il fait froid.
It's windy. Il fait du vent.
What's the weather like? Quel temps fait-il?

Revision exercises 1

Exercise 1

Example:
you / Mike / teacher
— Who are you?
— I'm Mike. I'm a teacher.

1. she / Miss Brown / secretary
2. they / Bill and Pete / mechanics
3. he / Jack / farmer
4. you / Mary / receptionist
5. she / Mrs Green / doctor
6. they / Mike and John / teachers

Exercise 2

Example:
567 9840
Hello, five six seven, nine eight four "0".

1. 688 4237
2. 333 7965
3. 871 9054
4. 506 2232
5. 899 6410

Exercise 3

Complete the sentences with prepositions.

1. Mr and Mrs Carter are ... holiday.
2. Uncle Bob's ... his shop.
3. Miss Smart's ... the beach.
4. Pam's ... home.
5. Mr and Mrs Black are ... Italy.
6. Mike's ... front ... the supermarket.

Exercise 4

Example:
the dinner / nice (No)
— Is the dinner nice?
— No, it isn't.

1. Italy / nice (Yes)
2. the beach / dirty (Yes)
3. Dave's shoes / blue (No)
4. Jenny's car / red (Yes)
5. the keys / in your pocket (No)
6. the cinema / near the supermarket (Yes)

Exercise 5

Example:
this / your shop (Yes)
— Is this your shop?
— Yes, it is.

1. these / his parcels (Yes)
2. this / your sister (Yes)
3. those / her parents (No)
4. that / our camera (Yes)
5. those / their friends (No)
6. this / my ticket (Yes)

Exercise 6

Example:
desk / Rosie
— Whose desk is this?
— It's Rosie's desk.

1. apples / Dave
2. hat / Charlie
3. house / Mr and Mrs Carter
4. tickets / Miss Smart
5. cup / Uncle Bob
6. basket / Jenny

Exercise 7

Complete the sentences with "whose" or "who's":

1. "... Dave?" "He's my brother."
2. "... car is that?" "It's Mike's car."
3. "... keys are these?" "They're my keys."
4. "... Mr Carter?" "He's my Dad."
5. "... Jenny?" "She's Mike's wife."
6. "... bag is this?" "It's Mrs Carter's bag."

Exercise 8

Complete the sentences with "keys, books, car, tickets, pen" and a preposition.

1. The ... are ... my pocket.
2. Our ...'s ... the car park.
3. My ...'s ... the table.
4. Her ... are ... her bag.
5. Their ... are ... the floor.

Exercise 9

Complete the sentences with "what, how, where, who" or "why".

1. "...'s your dog?" "He's fine, thank you."
2. "...'s London?" "It's in England."
3. "... are those?" "They're Arthur's bones."
4. "... are my socks?" "They're under the chair."
5. "... time is it, please?"
6. "... isn't he here?" "Because he's at school."
7. "...'s Mike Carter?" "He's my brother."
8. "...'s the weather like in Italy?"

Revision exercises 1

Crossword

Across

1. It's ... and sunny.
4. Please ... quiet!
5. "Where's Arthur?" "Look! He's ... there."
7. Here's Mrs Carter. Look at ... car!
8. Pam ... Dave are very nice.
11. "Is this your ...?" "Yes, and that's my sock too."
13. "Is it good?" "..., it isn't."
14. "Where's ... car park?"

Down

1. "Where's the light switch?" "... it is!"
2. "Rosie's at home." "Is Dave at home ...?"
3. "Excuse ... . What time is it?"
6. "What colour's Charlie's hat?" "It's ... ."
7. Uncle Bob's in ... shop.
9. Four + five = ...
10. Mr Carter's a ... .
12. "Is Dave ready?" "Yes, ... is."

Exercises

1. *Example:*
small dog
Good heavens! What a small dog!

1. big car park
2. heavy chairs
3. difficult exercise
4. strong boys
5. nice garden
6. hot day

2. *Example:*
his car / big
— Look at his car! It's very big, isn't it?
— Yes, it is.

1. their camera / expensive
2. my teeth / dirty
3. Arthur's tongue / dirty
4. my brother / brown
5. Mike Carter / strong
6. the weather / sunny

3. *Example:*
Rosie / quiet
— Oh dear! Rosie isn't very quiet, is she?
— No, she isn't.

1. his records / good
2. Pam / well
3. the headmaster / friendly
4. the boots / cheap
5. Mrs Carter / happy
6. the beach / nice

4. *Example:*
Dave's camera / good
— Is Dave's camera good?
— Yes, it's a very good camera.

1. Pam's records / good
2. his flat / small
3. the shop over there / cheap
4. the exercise / easy
5. your desk / heavy
6. Uncle Bob's dog / friendly

Summary of grammar

Adjectives

It's a	**difficult**	**exercise.**
They're		**exercises.**

Question-tags

I'm	**English,**	**aren't I?**
You're		**aren't you?**
He's		**isn't he?**
She's		**isn't she?**
It's		**isn't it?**
We're		**aren't we?**
You're		**aren't you?**
They're		**aren't they?**

I'm not	**English,**	**am I?**
You aren't		**are you?**
He isn't		**is he?**
She isn't		**is she?**
It isn't		**is it?**
We aren't		**are we?**
You aren't		**are you?**
They aren't		**are they?**

6

Notes de grammaire

1. **An expensive book.** Un livre cher.
   Two expensive books. Deux livres chers.
   An expensive car. Une voiture chère.
   Two expensive cars. Deux voitures chères.

L'adjectif qualificatif épithète se place toujours avant le nom. Souvenez-vous qu'en anglais, les adjectifs (épithètes et attributs) sont invariables.

2. **He's strong, isn't he?** Il est fort, n'est-ce pas?
   He isn't strong, is he? Il n'est pas fort, n'est-ce pas?

Les expressions comme « isn't he? — are you? — aren't we? etc. » s'appellent « question-tags ». La « question-tag » s'emploie à toutes les personnes. Lorsque le verbe est à la forme affirmative, la « question-tag » est à la forme interro-négative. Lorsque le verbe est à la forme négative, la « question-tag » est à la forme interrogative.

Notez les question-tags de la 1re personne du singulier du verbe « to be » :

I'm strong, aren't I?
I'm not very strong, am I?

3. **What a big dog!** Quel grand chien!
   What big dogs! Quels grands chiens!

Remarquez la présence de l'article indéfini dans la phrase exclamative au singulier.

Vocabulaire

boy garçon
headmaster proviseur
object objet
oil huile
rope corde
sea mer
teeth (tooth) dents (dent)
tongue langue
water eau

big grand / gros
difficult difficile
easy facile
expensive cher
friendly amical
heavy lourd
polluted pollué
poor pauvre
similar pareil
small petit
strong fort

with avec

to come venir
to draw dessiner
to make faire / fabriquer
to wait attendre
to watch regarder

Be careful! Fais / Faites attention!
Good heavens! Mon dieu!

Quatrième page

boot botte
clock horloge / pendule
everything tout

cheap bon marché

How much? Combien?
They're only a pound.
Ils ne coûtent qu'une livre.

Exercises

1. *Example:*
you / read a book
— What are you doing?
— I'm reading a book.

1. she / play the piano
2. he / make a boat
3. they / work in the garden
4. Mr and Mrs Carter / watch television
5. you and Pam / do our exercises
6. those people / look at the sea

2. *Example:*
Mr Carter / go to the cinema (Mrs Carter)
— Mr Carter's going to the cinema.
Is Mrs Carter going to the cinema too?
— Yes, she is.

1. Charlie / stand in front of the supermarket (Dave and Pam)
2. Uncle Bob / sit on the beach (Arthur)
3. Mike and Jenny / walk along the street (Tim and Tony)
4. Miss Smart / have dinner (Mr and Mrs Carter)
5. Mr Carter / do the housework (Mike)
6. Dave / look out of the window (Rosie)

3. *Example:*
man / jump out of the window
Look at that man! He's jumping out of the window.

1. woman / wear my red trousers
2. boy / sit on my motorbike
3. teachers / all carry pink and white umbrellas
4. policeman / stand in your garden
5. people / all go into our classroom
6. boys / watch Mr Hardy, the headmaster

4. *Example:*
cold / you / coat
It's cold. Why aren't you wearing a coat?

1. windy / he / pullover
2. sunny / she / sunglasses
3. raining / you / raincoat
4. cold / they / scarves
5. hot / he / hat
6. raining / they / boots

Summary of grammar

Present continuous

What	am I are you is he are we are you are they	doing?

I'm You're He's We're You're They're	reading.

Am I Are you Is he Are we Are you Are they	reading?

Yes,	I am. you are. he is. we are. you are. they are.

No,	I'm not. you aren't. he isn't. we aren't. you aren't. they aren't.

Contractions

I'm reading.	I am reading.
He's reading.	He is reading.
They're reading.	They are reading.

7

Notes de grammaire

1. He's reading. Il lit (en ce moment).

Le « present continuous » (le présent progressif) sert à exprimer des actions en cours.

2. Attention à l'orthographe de ces verbes au « present continuous » :

To make; I'm making.
To come; I'm coming.
To sit; I'm sitting.

3. Ne confondez pas « to make » et « to do » :

To do + the washing-up / an exercise / the housework.
To make + a noise / a dress / a film.

4. Look at that! Regarde cà!
Look at those! Regarde ceux-là!
Look at that woman! Regarde cette femme-là!
Look at those people! Regarde ces gens-là!

« That, those » (et « this, these ») sont adjectifs aussi bien que pronoms démonstratifs.

N.B. « People », quand il signifie « les gens », est toujours accompagné du pluriel.

Vocabulaire

afternoon après-midi
bedroom chambre à coucher
boat bateau
dress robe
everyone tout le monde
housework ménage
kitchen cuisine
living-room salle de séjour
man homme
noise bruit
people gens
woman femme

all tout(e), tous, toutes
full of plein de / rempli de
incredible incroyable
pretty joli

along le long de
(to walk along the street marcher dans la rue**)**

into dans
out of de
(out of the window par la fenêtre**)**

to do faire
to do the washing-up faire la vaiselle
to jump sauter
to make a film tourner un film
to play jouer
to read lire
to sit s'asseoir
to stand se tenir debout
to walk marcher
to watch television regarder la télévision
to work travailler

What's happening? Que se passe-t-il?

Quatrième page

coat manteau
electric fire radiateur électrique
raincoat imperméable
scarf foulard / écharpe
shirt chemise
skirt jupe
sunglasses lunettes de soleil
trousers pantalon

today aujourd'hui

to carry porter
to wear porter (un vêtement)

It's raining. Il pleut.

Exercises

1. *Example:*
you / wait / your friend (Yes)
— Are you waiting for your friend?
— Yes, I am.

1. Sergeant Salt / talk / Constable Potter (Yes)
2. Mr Hardy / listen / the radio (No)
3. Arthur / wait / his dinner (Yes)
4. You / look / the camera (No)
5. The air-hostess / talk / the people (No)
6. Mike and Jenny / listen / the announcement (Yes)

2. *Example:*
Look / that car
— Hey, Dave! Look at that car!
— I'm looking at it!

1. listen / that noise
2. wait / me
3. look / all those people
4. wait / us
5. listen / the doctor
6. look / that pretty woman

3. *Example:*
what / wait
Hurry up! What are you waiting for?

1. what / look
2. who / wait
3. what / listen
4. who / look
5. who / talk

4. *Example:*
Eat your dinner! (Arthur)
Arthur's eating it.

1. Talk to Pam! (Charlie)
2. Ask Mr and Mrs Carter! (Rosie)
3. Pull the rope! (Uncle Bob)
4. Go with Dave! (Rosie)
5. Do the washing-up! (Mike)
6. Stand behind Jenny! (Mrs Carter)

Summary of grammar

Verb + preposition

She's talking.	**Who's she talking to?**
She's listening.	**What's she listening to?**
She's waiting.	**What's she waiting for?**
She's looking.	**What's she looking at?**

Object pronouns

She's	**talking to** **listening to** **waiting for** **looking at**	**me.** **you.** **him, her, it.** **us.** **you.** **them.**

8

Notes de grammaire

1. **He's waiting.** Il attend.
   What's he waiting for? Qu'est-ce qu'il attend?
   He's waiting for the bus. Il attend l'autobus.

Le complément de certains verbes est toujours introduit par une préposition : « to look at — to wait for — to listen to ». Dans les phrases interrogatives, cette préposition reste après le verbe.

2. **I'm reading it.** Je le lis.
   She's looking at him. Elle le regarde.
   He's talking to them. Il leur parle.

Les pronoms personnels compléments (it, him, etc.) sont toujours placés après le verbe qu'ils complètent.

3. **His garage is in Park Street.**
   Their house is over there.
   The beach is dirty.
   This is Pam.
   The air-hostess is talking.

Notez qu'après les mots qui se terminent par « ge, se, ch, sh, s, x » on n'emploie pas la forme contractée de « is ». On écrit et prononce la forme complète [iz].

4. **Attention à l'orthographe :**
   To get out; I'm getting out.

Vocabulaire

air-hostess hôtesse de l'air
airport aéroport
announcement annonce
balloon ballon
bus-stop arrêt d'autobus
cow vache
information information(s)
nothing rien
plane avion
police car voiture de police
report rapport
sky ciel
station gare
tree arbre
wind vent

fast vite

too (big) trop (grand)

to eat manger
to get out sortir / descendre
to go down descendre
to go home rentrer à la maison
to listen to écouter
to pull tirer
to say dire
to talk to parler à

It's foggy. Il y a du brouillard.
It's making me ill. Cela me rend malade.

Chanson : page 43

letter lettre
newspaper journal

Revision exercises 2

Exercise 1

Example:
Pam / brother / Dave
Hello, my name's Pam. This is my brother, Dave.

1. Dave / friend / Charlie
2. Mr Carter / wife / Marion
3. Charlie / uncle / Mr Kipper
4. Rosie / parents / Mr and Mrs Carter
5. Mr Kipper / dog / Arthur
6. Dave / sisters / Rosie and Pam
7. Tim / teacher / Mr Carter

Exercise 2

Example:
he / at school today
— Is he at school today?
— Yes, he is.

1. it / cold today (No)
2. they / at the airport (Yes)
3. Mike Carter / a sports teacher (Yes)
4. he / at Tim's house (No)
5. she / your sister (Yes)
6. that / our plane to Paris (No)
7. you and Dave / ready (No)
8. it / three o'clock (Yes)
9. Mike and Jenny / on holiday (No)
10. Pam / on the beach (Yes)

Exercise 3

Example:
small boy
What a small boy! Look at him!

1. big cow
2. small apples
3. pretty air-hostess
4. strong policeman
5. friendly politicians

Exercise 4

Complete the sentences with "in, on, into, at, out of, behind, in front of, along, under."

1. Why isn't Dave ... school today?
2. Look at Arthur! He's jumping ... the boat!
3. Be careful! Sergeant Salt's ... you.
4. Rosie's walking ... Park Street with her friend.
5. Hey! You're standing ... my foot!
6. "Where are my socks?" "They're ... the bed."
7. Uncle Bob's going ... his shop.
8. Oh dear! My keys aren't ... my pocket.
9. There's Charlie. He's standing ... the cinema.

Exercise 5

Example:
pen / this / Mr Carter
— Whose pen is this?
— It's Mr Carter's pen, isn't it?

1. umbrella / that / Miss Smart
2. bones / those / Arthur
3. basket / this / Jenny
4. socks / these / Dave
5. parcel / that / Uncle Bob

Exercise 6

Complete the passage with "to work, to watch, to make, to come, to do (2), to stand, to carry, to play, to walk."

It's Tuesday afternoon. What's everyone ...? Well, Charlie's ... in his garage. He's under a red car and he's very dirty! Uncle Bob's ... at the door of his shop. He's ... the people in the street. Arthur's very happy. He's ... two big bones into the garden. Where's Mrs Carter? Oh, there she is, in the supermarket. She's ... the shopping. And here's Sergeant Salt. He's ... along the street with Constable Potter. Mike Carter's at school. He's ... football with the boys in his class. But Mr Hardy's ... because they're ... a noise!

Exercise 7

Example:
Her coat isn't white. It's black.

1. That house isn't big. It's ... .
2. Those shoes aren't expensive. They're ... .
3. It isn't hot today. It's ... .
4. This exercise isn't difficult. It's ... .

Exercise 8

Complete the dialogue.

A: ...
B: Hello, A. ...
A: I'm fine, thank you.
B: ...
A: I'm going to the shops. ...
B: ...
A: To the cinema! That's nice.
B: ... with me!
A: Sorry. My mother's over there, and she's waiting for me.

Revision exercises 2

Exercise 9

Pronunciation
One word is different. Can you find it?

1. good / look / boot
2. home / come / bone
3. here / there / where
4. rain / wait / chair
5. heavy / cheap / beach

Exercise 10

Complete the passage with prepositions.

Jenny's ... the beach. She's waiting ... Mike. She's looking ... all the people near her. A small boy's watching two dogs ... the sea. A man's talking ... his wife. But she isn't listening ... him because she's reading a magazine. Jenny's looking ... the time. It's half ... five. It's cold now, and everyone's going home. Where's Mike?

Exercise 11

Where's the stress in these words?
Example: **dinner: dinner**

1. airport
2. bedroom
3. guitar
4. garden
5. surprise
6. report
7. kitchen
8. magazine
9. birthday
10. along

Exercise 12

These sentences are the answers to questions. Make the questions.

Example:
Jenny's on the beach.
Where's Jenny?

1. It's half past eight.
2. He isn't very well today.
3. Your football boots are in the kitchen, Dave.
4. My name's Tony.
5. It's sunny but it's very windy.
6. Miss Smart's car's green.
7. Dave isn't doing the washing-up because he's watching television.
8. They're going to the station.
9. That's my brother, Tim.
10. It's Charlie's motorbike.

Exercise 13

What are these words?

Example: **ARC** = **CAR**

GBA ATOB UTB LAL NAD DWINY YODAT ROTOKEBIM STERE TOBO

Exercise 14

Complete the sentences with question-tags.

1. Mr Carter's doing the washing-up, ...
2. Jenny and Mike are going home, ...
3. I'm not coming, ...
4. He isn't listening to us, ...
5. We're going very fast, ...
6. You aren't getting out, ...

Exercise 15

Contractions
Example:
Uncle Bob is green!
Uncle Bob's green!

1. We are listening to the announcement.
2. He is getting out of the balloon.
3. It is making him ill.
4. I am waiting for my friend.
5. They are not going with him.
6. You are not talking, are you?

Exercises

1. *Example:*
we / watch television
— Can we watch television, please?
— Yes, of course you can.

1. I / taste it
2. they / listen to your records
3. you / wait for me
4. we / go home now
5. she / read that newspaper
6. I / wear your raincoat

2. *Example:*
you / not see me
You can't see me, can you?

1. Mrs Carter / not hear the bell
2. Uncle Bob / sing very well
3. you / cook
4. the vet / not come this afternoon
5. Tim and Tony / sit in the front row
6. we / not open the parcel

3. *Example:*
I'm cold. (my scarf)
I'm cold. Can you give me my scarf, please?

1. She isn't very well. (an aspirin)
2. Arthur's in the kitchen. (a bone)
3. Those girls are waiting for you, Miss Smart. (a job)
4. I'm going to the airport now. (my ticket)
5. Sergeant Salt and Constable Potter are here. (their instructions)
6. The air-hostess is doing the washing-up. (the dirty cups)

4. *Example:*
I / move the piano / heavy
I can't move the piano because it's too heavy.

1. I / eat this ice-cream / cold
2. he / do that exercise / difficult
3. they / go into the sea / dirty
4. we / move this table / big
5. I / go to London / foggy
6. you / give her that bag / expensive

Summary of grammar

« Can »

Can	I you he we you they	go now? see? cook?

Yes,	I you he we you they	can.

No,	I you he we you they	can't.

Contraction

can't	cannot

« Give + object pronoun + noun »

Miss Smart can give	me you him her us you them	a job.

9

Notes de grammaire

1. **Can you see him?** Est-ce que tu peux le voir? / Le vois-tu?
   Can I go, please? Puis-je m'en aller, s'il vous plaît?

« Can » exprime la possibilité et sert aussi à demander la permission de faire quelque chose.

Can you cook? Sais-tu faire la cuisine?
Can you play the piano? Sais-tu jouer du piano?

Il exprime aussi la capacité de faire quelque chose; il a le sens du verbe français « savoir ».

N.B. « Can » est suivi de l'infinitif sans « to ».

2. **I can give Pam a job.** Je peux offrir un poste à Pam.
   I can give her a job. Je peux lui offrir un poste.

Attention à l'ordre des mots. Le complément d'attribution (Pam / her) se met tout de suite après le verbe et avant le complément d'objet direct (a job).

3. **Notez les « question-tags » de « can ».**

   She can cook, can't she? Elle sait faire la cuisine, n'est-ce pas?
   He can't come, can he? Il ne peut pas venir, n'est-ce pas?

4. **Attention à l'orthographe :**

   To give; he's giving.
   To move; they're moving.

Vocabulaire

bath baignoire / bain
bell sonnette
cook cuisinier
employment agency bureau d'embauche
evening soir
front row premier rang
ice-cream glace
office bureau

Chinese Chinois
dressed habillé
other autre

so alors / donc

to cook cuisiner
to get dressed s'habiller
to give donner
to hear entendre
to look for chercher
to move bouger
to open ouvrir
to ring sonner
to see voir
to sing chanter

I can je peux

Of course. Bien sûr.
You're looking for a job then?
Vous cherchez un emploi, alors?

Exercises

1. *Example:*
an ambulance in the street
There's an ambulance in the street, isn't there?

1. a big hole in the roof
2. two fire-engines in front of the supermarket
3. a teacher in the front row
4. three policemen on the corner
5. a small factory in Brighton
6. four firemen outside

2. *Example:*
people / upstairs
How many people are there upstairs?

1. towns / in England
2. clocks / in Miss Smart's office
3. trees / in the garden
4. people / in the front row
5. bus-stops / in your street
6. maps / on the desk

3. *Example:*
dog in the garden (Yes)
— Is there a dog in the garden?
— Yes, there is.

1. Chinese Restaurant in this town (No)
2. eight people in that car (Yes)
3. taxi in front of the cinema (No)
4. Information Office at the airport (Yes)
5. two planes to Paris today (No)
6. employment agency in Park Street (Yes)

4. *Complete the sentences with « Let's » or « Don't ».*

1. ... see that film. It isn't very good.
2. It's a nice day. ... eat outside.
3. ... play your guitar. I'm listening to the radio.
4. ... watch television this evening. There's a good film.
5. It's very late. ... make a noise!
6. ... open that parcel. It isn't for you.

Summary of grammar

« There is, are »

There's an ambulance There are two ambulances	in the street.

Is there an ambulance	in the street?	Yes, there is. No, there isn't.
Are there two ambulances		Yes, there are. No, there aren't.

Imperative

Go home, Pam! Let's go home! Go home, Pam and Dave!	Don't go home, Pam! Let's not go home! Don't go home, Pam and Dave!

Contractions

Don't	Do not
Let's	Let us

10

Notes de grammaire

1. **There's a doctor here.** Il y a un médecin ici.
   There are two doctors here. Il y a deux médecins ici.

Notez l'expression « there is » — pluriel « there are ».

There's a living-room, three bedrooms, and a big kitchen.

Attention! Si le premier mot d'une liste de mots est au singulier, on emploie « there is ».

Notez les « question-tags » :

There isn't a map on the table, is there?
There are two cookers, aren't there?

2. **Come here, Pam!** Viens ici, Pam!
   Come here, Pam and Dave! Venez ici, Pam et Dave!
   Don't talk , Pam! Ne parle pas, Pam!
   Don't talk, Pam and Dave! Ne parlez pas, Pam et Dave!

La deuxième personne de l'impératif a la même forme au singulier et au pluriel.

Let's go, Mike! Allons-y, Mike!

La première personne du pluriel de l'impératif se forme avec « let's » (let us) et l'infinitif sans « to ».

3. **A man; two men.**

Faites attention à ce pluriel irrégulier.

4. **Mike and Jenny's address.** L'adresse de Mike et Jenny.
   Pam and Dave's brother. Le frère de Pam et Dave.

En général, quand il y a deux possesseurs, le « 's » du cas possessif ne s'ajoute qu'au deuxième.

Vocabulaire

address adresse
cooker cuisinière
corner coin
factory usine
fire-engine voiture de pompiers
fireman (firemen) pompier(s)
hole trou
house agent agent immobilier
map carte
park parc
photograph photographie
photographer photographe
postcard carte postale
roof toit
room salle / pièce
someone quelqu'un
(a) thousand mille
town centre centre ville

enormous énorme
old vieux

always toujours
outside dehors
upstairs en haut

to spell épeler
to take prendre
to write écrire

for sale à vendre
Dear John... Cher John...
How many? Combien?
Love from... Amitiés de...
The supermarket's on fire. Le supermarché a pris feu.

11

Exercises

1. *Example:*
chicken / fridge / butter
There's some chicken in the fridge, but there isn't any butter.

1. salt / pie / pepper
2. women / swimming-pool / men
3. old books / shop / old clothes
4. carrots / basket / onions
5. sandwiches / kitchen / ice-cream
6. keys / my pocket / money

2. *Example:*
chicken / kitchen / table
— Is there any chicken in the kitchen?
— Yes, there's a lot of chicken on the table.

1. junk / the Carter's house / garage
2. new flats / Brighton / Green Street
3. instructions / book / front page
4. tomatoes / kitchen / fridge
5. good books / your room / table
6. nice shops / Brighton / town centre

3. *Complete the sentences with « any », « some », « a » or « an »:*

1. The politician's talking to ... policemen.
2. Don't eat ... onions.
3. Let's make ... sandwiches.
4. There's ... ambulance in front of his house.
5. Oh dear! There aren't ... tickets for the football match.
6. I can't see ... planes in the sky.
7. « What's the matter? » « There are ... dirty socks in my pocket. »
8. There's ... swimming-pool in his garden.
9. Give me ... bones for Arthur, please.
10. There's ... enormous dog under my bed!
11. Are there ... good films on television?
12. Her husband's looking for ... new job.

Summary of grammar

« Some, any »

There's	**some**	**butter**	**in the fridge.**
There are		**carrots**	

There isn't	**any**	**butter**	**in the fridge.**
There aren't		**carrots**	

Is there	**any**	**butter**	**in the fridge?**
Are there		**carrots**	

11

Notes de grammaire

1. **Is there any chicken?** Y a-t-il du poulet?
   No, there isn't any chicken. Non, il n'y a pas de poulet.
   But there are some carrots. Mais il y a des carottes.

« Some » et « any » expriment la même chose : une certaine quantité ou un certain nombre. Ils s'emploient avec des noms « indénombrables » — qu'on ne peut pas compter (pepper, salt, butter) ou des noms pluriels (onions, carrots, tomatoes).

On emploie « some » dans les phrases affirmatives et « any » dans les phrases négatives et la plupart des phrases interrogatives.

They're wearing coats. Ils portent un manteau.
There are some coats in the cupboard. Il y a des manteaux dans le placard.

Faites attention à la différence entre ces deux phrases. « Some » sert à exprimer un certain nombre.

2. **There's a lot of pepper.** Il y a beaucoup de poivre.
   There are a lot of onions. Il y a beaucoup d'oignons.

« A lot of » s'emploie avec des noms indénombrables et des noms pluriels.

3. **Attention à l'orthographe :**

A woman; two women.
A tomato; two tomatoes.
To take; I'm taking.

Vocabulaire

butter beurre
carrot carotte
chicken poulet
chicken pie poulet en croûte
clothes vêtements
day jour/journée
fridge (refrigerator) « frigo » (réfrigérateur)
husband mari
junk brocante
lunch déjeuner
money argent
onion oignon
pepper poivre
salt sel
swimming-pool piscine
tomato tomate

bad mauvais
new neuf/nouveau
surprised surpris
true vrai

to burn brûler

Here you are! Tiens!/Tenez!
on television à la télévision
What's the matter? Qu'est-ce qu'il y a?

12

Exercises

1. *Make questions and give true answers.*
Example:
Miss Smart / yellow bikini
— Has Miss Smart got a yellow bikini?
— Yes, she has.

1. you / pink toothbrush
2. Mr Carter / moustache
3. your teacher / black hair
4. Mr and Mrs Carter / big house
5. your house / blue door
6. Pam / new job

2. *Example:*
you / matches
— You haven't got any matches, have you?
— No, I haven't.

1. Mike and Jenny / big flat
2. she / brothers
3. you / new job
4. he / red shirt
5. Sergeant Salt / very nice office
6. we / money

3. *Example:*
a postcard of Brighton
— Can I have a postcard of Brighton, please?
— I'm sorry. We haven't got any postcards of Brighton.

1. a pink ice-cream
2. a green pen
3. a blue and yellow umbrella
4. a bone for Arthur
5. two tickets for this evening
6. an apple

4. *Example:*
you / make a fish pie / cooker
You can't make a fish pie because you haven't got a cooker.

1. the photographer / take a photo / camera
2. I / eat my dinner / knife and fork
3. Mrs Carter / go to town / car
4. Pam and I / open the door / key
5. I / write this postcard / pen
6. Dave and Charlie / go to the football match / tickets

Summary of grammar

« Have got »

I've You've He's We've You've They've	got	a ticket.

I haven't You haven't He hasn't We haven't You haven't They haven't	got	a ticket.

Have I Have you Has he Have we Have you Have they	got	a ticket?

Yes,	I have. you have. he has. we have. you have. they have.

No,	I haven't. you haven't. he hasn't. we haven't. you haven't. they haven't.

He's got a ticket, hasn't he? He hasn't got a ticket, has he?
They've got a ticket, haven't they? They haven't got a ticket, have they?

Contractions

I've got	I have got
He's got	He has got
I haven't got	I have not got
He hasn't got	He has not got

Notes de grammaire

1. **I have got a knife.**
   I have a knife. } J'ai un couteau.

« Have got » et « have » expriment la possession, mais « have got » est beaucoup plus fréquent en anglais moderne.

I've got a knife. J'ai un couteau.
Can I have a fork? Puis-je avoir une fourchette?

« Have got » ne s'emploie pas à l'infinitif. On emploie « have » (infinitif sans « to ») après « can ».

2. **Charlie's got a motorbike, but I haven't.** Charlie a une moto, mais pas moi.

Il n'est pas nécessaire de répéter « got a motorbike » : il suffit d'employer l'auxiliaire « haven't ».

3. **Attention à la traduction de « have » dans les phrases comme :**

To have dinner. Dîner.
To have lunch. Déjeuner.

Ici, « have » a le sens de « prendre ».

4. **She's got long hair.** Elle a les cheveux longs.
   Her hair is brown. Ses cheveux sont bruns.

N.B. « hair » est singulier.

Vocabulaire

box boîte
chemist pharmacien
customer client
fish poisson
fork fourchette
knife couteau
match allumette
police station commissariat de police
toothbrush brosse à dents
shelf étagère / rayon
wallet portefeuille

yourself toi-même / vous-même

interesting intéressant

to empty vider
to help aider
to question interroger

Certainly! Certainement!
Just a minute! Attends / Attendez une minute!
the top shelf le rayon du haut
Yes, sir. Oui, monsieur.

Quatrième page

glasses lunettes
hair cheveux
notice pancarte / avis

fat gros
quite assez
short petit / court
tall grand
thin mince

What's he like? Comment est-il?

Exercises

1. *Example:*
Mrs Carter's doing the housework. (every morning)
Yes, she does the housework every morning.

1. Charlie's working in his garage. (every day)
2. Miss Smart's listening to the radio. (every evening)
3. Rosie and Dave are having a cup of tea. (every morning)
4. Mr Carter's going to London. (every Monday)
5. You're waiting for the bus. (every afternoon)
6. Mrs Carter's washing the car. (every Sunday)

2. *Example:*
Dave goes to school by bus. (Rosie)
— Does Rosie go to school by bus, too?
— Yes, she does.

1. We want to see the match. (you)
2. Uncle Bob sings in the bath. (Charlie)
3. Dave likes football. (Tim and Tony)
4. Mr Carter speaks French. (Mrs Carter)
5. My car makes a noise. (your car)
6. Maria comes from Italy. (Carlo)

3. *Example:*
they / get up at six on Sunday
— They don't get up at six on Sunday, do they?
— No, of course they don't.

1. the cooks / finish work at midnight every night
2. Mike / speak Chinese
3. Mrs Carter / stay in bed on Sunday
4. you / go to school by car
5. Pam Carter / wear glasses
6. Sergeant Salt / want to watch this film

4. *Can you complete these sentences?*

1. Sergeant Salt drives ... Brighton in his car every Saturday night.
2. What time do you get ...?
3. The house is ... fire! Jump ... ... the window!
4. « Can you give me a lift? » « Certainly. Get ...! »
5. What does Mr Carter do ... Sunday morning?
6. Do you go ... school ... bus?

Summary of grammar

Simple present

I get up You get up He gets up We get up You get up They get up	at seven.

I don't You don't He doesn't We don't You don't They don't	get up at seven.

Do I Do you Does he Do we Do you Do they	get up at seven?

Yes,	I do. you do. he does. we do. you do. they do.

No,	I don't. you don't. he doesn't. we don't. you don't. they don't.

You get up at seven, don't you? You don't get up at seven, do you?
He gets up at seven, doesn't he? He doesn't get up at seven, does he?

Contractions

don't	do not
doesn't	does not

13

Notes de grammaire

1. **He's getting up (now).** Il se lève (en ce moment).
   He gets up at seven (every day). Il se lève à sept heures (tous les jours).

Remarquez la différence entre les deux formes du présent. Le présent simple exprime en anglais des actions habituelles. Le présent progressif (present continuous) exprime des actions en cours.

2. **I get up at seven.**
   He gets up at half past seven.

Attention! La 3ᵉ personne du singulier du présent simple (he, she, it) prend un « s ».

3. **I like this coffee.** J'aime ce café.
   I want a ticket. Je veux un billet.

Les verbes « to like, to want » s'emploient rarement à la forme progressive.

4. **Do you speak English?** Parlez-vous anglais?
   Be quiet! Don't talk! Silence! Ne parlez pas!

« To speak » et « to talk » ont tous les deux le sens de « parler ». On emploie « to speak » quand il s'agit de parler une langue.

5. **She works from two to six.** Elle travaille de deux heures à six heures.

La suppression de « o'clock » est assez fréquente.

6. **Attention à l'orthographe :**

   I do; he does.
   I go; he goes.
   I wash; he washes.
   I finish; he finishes.

Vocabulaire

bed lit
breakfast petit déjeuner
coffee café
day jour
midnight minuit
night nuit
road chemin / route
surgery cabinet (de médecin)
tea thé

French Français

round autour de / dans
by (car) en (voiture)

to drive conduire
to find trouver
to finish finir
to get in monter dans (une voiture)
to get up se lever
to give someone a lift prendre quelqu'un en voiture
prendre quelqu'un qui fait de l'auto-stop

to like aimer
to speak parler
to stay rester
to want vouloir
to wash laver

every day tous les jours
on Sunday Dimanche / le dimanche

Exercises

1. *Example:*
Arthur / sleep outside / usually
Arthur usually sleeps outside.

1. Dave / wash his hair / never
2. Mike and Jenny / come home late / often
3. my husband / drink coffee at breakfast / usually
4. the headmaster / drop his glasses / often
5. we / have breakfast in bed / sometimes
6. he / drop ash on the floor / always

2. *Example:*
the agent / go to Brighton / often (London)
— Does the agent ever go to Brighton?
— No, he never goes to Brighton, but he often goes to London.

1. they / win the Boat Race / usually (Car Rally)
2. Miss Smart / work on Sunday / always (Saturday)
3. she / go to Italy on holiday / sometimes (France)
4. Arthur / sleep on the beach / often (garden)
5. you / drink tea / sometimes (coffee)
6. Uncle Bob / listen to records / often (radio)

3. *Example:*
radio / Miss Smart's winning (incredible)
— The radio says Miss Smart's winning.
— I know she is. I think she's incredible.

1. instructions / it isn't easy (too difficult)
2. newspaper / they're first in the race (very good)
3. Dave / Charlie's very friendly (really nice)
4. programme / she sings in Chinese (incredible)
5. air-hostess / the weather's bad (too foggy)
6. this magazine / the sea's polluted (very dirty)

4. *Examples:*
tea (every morning)
— Do you like tea?
— Yes, I do. I have tea every morning.

English records (two / at home)
— Do you like English records?
— Yes, I do. I've got two English records at home.

1. dogs (three / at home)
2. English magazines (some / in my desk)
3. fish (often / for lunch)
4. blue sails (two / on my boat)
5. apples (an apple every day)
6. coffee (every morning at breakfast)

Summary of grammar

Frequency adverbs

Do they	always usually often sometimes ever	win?

They	always usually often sometimes never	win.

They don't	always usually often	win.

Are they	usually ever	first?

They're	always never	first.

They aren't	usually often	first.

14

Notes de grammaire

1. **Does Bob always sing in the bath?**
   I don't usually come home late.

Les adverbes de temps « always, usually, sometimes, never, often » se placent devant le verbe (sing, come).

He's never first.

Ils se placent après « to be ».

2. **I think (that) it's got red sails.**
   Je pense qu'il a des voiles rouges.
   The programme says (that) it's number forty-six.
   Le programme dit que c'est le numéro quarante-six.

En anglais, la conjonction « that » est souvent sous-entendue. Cela ne change pas le sens de la phrase.

3. **Do you like coffee?** Aimes-tu le café?
   Do you like tomatoes? Aimes-tu les tomates?

Ici l'absence d'article indique que l'on parle du café, des tomates en général.

4. **I think we're winning. We <u>are</u> winning!**

Notez que dans la deuxième phrase on emploie la forme complète de « are » qui est accentué pour montrer la surprise de celui qui parle.

Vocabulaire

ash cendre
flag drapeau
food nourriture
front door porte d'entrée
number numéro
person personne
race course
regatta régate
sail voile
year an / année

tonight ce soir

first premier
last dernier

ever jamais
never ne ... jamais
often souvent
sometimes quelquefois
usually habituellement / d'habitude / en général

to close fermer
to drink boire
to drop laisser tomber / faire tomber
to know savoir
to live vivre / habiter
to go out sortir
to sleep dormir
to think penser
to win gagner

Come on! Viens! / Venez! / Allons-y!
There it is! Le / La voilà!

Revision exercises 3

Exercise 1

Example:
he / work in London (Yes)
— Does he work in London?
— Yes, he does.

1. you / like carrots (No)
2. you and Pam / live in Brighton (Yes)
3. the cook / ever make chicken pies (Yes)
4. Mrs Carter / know Mr Hardy (No)
5. Mike and Jenny / speak French (No)
6. you / think it's cold today (Yes)
7. Danielle / come from France (Yes)
8. your sister / ever write to you (No)
9. they / often listen to English records (Yes)
10. it / rain every day in England (No)

Exercise 2

Constable Potter's watching Mr X; and he's talking to Sergeant Salt on his radio. This is Constable Potter's report.

"Mr X is coming out of his shop. He's walking along Green Street. He's going into the café on the corner. He's sitting at a table near the window. He's having a cup of tea. He's reading the newspaper. Now he's going out of the café. He's getting into his car. He's driving along Critton Street... He's getting out of his car in front of a small, blue house. He's walking to the house. He's opening the door. He's going into the house..."

Sergeant Salt isn't surprised, because Mr X does these things every day. Can you make a dialogue like this:

Constable Potter: Mr X is coming out of his shop.
Sergeant Salt: But, Constable Potter, he comes out of his shop every morning!

Exercise 3

Complete the dialogue.

A: Good morning, sir. ...
B: ... .
A: A box of matches? Certainly, sir.
B: ... .
A: Grove cigarettes? No, I'm sorry, we haven't.
B: ... .
A: Yes, sir, we have.
B: ... .
A: Two packets. ..., sir.
B: ... .
A: Ninety-four pence, please sir.
B: ... .
A: Thank you very much. Goodbye, sir.
B: ... .

Exercise 4

Example:
Mrs Carter / get up at seven (usually)
Mrs Carter usually gets up at seven.

1. Mike / give the French teacher a lift (often)
2. Rosie / cook the dinner on Saturday (sometimes)
3. Uncle Bob / drop his pipe in the bath (often)
4. Mr and Mrs Carter / go to Italy on holiday (usually)
5. Sergeant Salt / have tomato sandwiches for lunch (always)
6. Miss Smart / go to her office late (never)

Exercise 5

Stress: give the correct answer.

Example:
Does Mr Carter like coffee?
a. No, he likes tea.
b. No, he likes tea.
Answer: No, he likes tea.

1. Is it quarter to two?
a. No, it's quarter past two.
b. No, it's quarter past two.

2. Is Charlie wearing his hat?
a. No, he's carrying his hat.
b. No, he's carrying his hat.

3. Do you go to school by car?
a. No, I go to school by bus.
b. No, I go to school by bus.

4. Can Dave come on Saturday?
a. No, but Rosie can come on Saturday.
b. No, but Rosie can come on Saturday.

5. Are my glasses on the table?
a. No, they're under the table.
b. No, they're under the table.

Exercise 6

Example:
He's got glasses, (Yes)
— He's got glasses, hasn't he?
— Yes, he has.

1. You haven't got a programme, ... (Yes)
2. Brighton's got an enormous supermarket, ... (Yes)
3. He hasn't got a job, ... (No)
4. We haven't got any customers, ... (No)
5. She's got black hair, ... (Yes)
6. Look, that house hasn't got a roof, ... (No)

Exercise 7

What are these words?
Example: **LOCOHS: SCHOOL**

DBE RAHI CEEFFO YEK WNTO NMA MLFI NIEFK LEHO TLLWAE

Revision exercises 3

Exercise 8

Complete these sentences with "some", "any", or "a".

1. I can hear ... noise. What is it?
2. She's got ... money under her bed!
3. I don't want ... fish, thank you.
4. Have you got ... salt and pepper?
5. Why isn't he taking ... photos?
6. There isn't ... butter in my sandwich.

Exercise 9

Complete the sentences with question-tags.

Example:
It isn't cold, ...
It isn't cold, is it?

1. You can cook, ...
2. It's raining, ...
3. There's a new teacher at school, ...
4. They haven't got any money, ...
5. The boys are playing football, ...
6. Pam never eats fish, ...
7. That dog's very dirty, ...
8. You aren't going now, ...
9. Uncle Bob can't hear the bell, ...
10. Charlie's got a motorbike, ...
11. You like Brighton, ...
12. There aren't any apples in the basket, ...

Exercise 10

Find a word to complete these sentences.

1. I can't see. Where's the light ...?
2. Do you want a new job? Go to an ... .
3. Arthur's very dirty so Uncle Bob's ... him.
4. Excuse me! I'm first in this ... . You're behind me.
5. "Are there any cheap hotels in Brighton?" "I don't know. Go to the ... Office in the centre of town."
6. I want to take a photo of that plane. Where's my ...?
7. I can't move this heavy box. Can you ... me, please?
8. Uncle Bob's boat has got red ... .
9. "There's a lot of old ... in our garage." "Let's burn it."
10. I've got a knife but I haven't got a ... .

Exercise 11

Complete the sentences with the correct instruction (in the affirmative or negative form):
sleep, sit, get up, taste, wash, burn, give, be quiet.

1. ... that knife. It's dirty.
2. ... your fingers on that electric fire.
3. ... this chicken pie! Is it good?
4. Sssh! ...! It's very late. Everyone's in bed.
5. ... in that chair. There's a big hole in it.
6. ... in the kitchen tonight, Arthur. It's cold in the garden.
7. ...! It's half past eight.
8. ... him any ice-cream. It makes him ill.

Exercise 12

Answer these questions. Make true sentences about yourself.

1. What's your name?
2. How many people are there in your class at school?
3. Have you got any brothers or sisters?
4. What time do you usually go to bed?
5. What do you usually do in the evening?
6. What are you wearing today?
7. What are you doing now? Where are you sitting?
8. Do you think English is easy or difficult?

Exercises

1. *Example:*
camera / that (Dave)
— Whose camera's that?
— I think it's Dave's.

1. chicken pie / this (Charlie)
2. glasses / those (Rosie)
3. address / that (Uncle Bob)
4. socks / these (Dave)
5. cat / this (Mike and Jenny)
6. cases / those (Mr and Mrs Carter)

2. *Example:*
your bag / on the table
— That's your bag, isn't it?
— No, it isn't. Mine's on the table.

1. his newspaper / on the floor
2. our plane / over there
3. my programme / under the chair
4. your toothbrush / on the shelf
5. their telephone number / in the blue book
6. her nightdress / in the case

3. *Example:*
That's my wallet.
That wallet's mine. Can you give it to me, please?

1. Those are our tomato sandwiches.
2. This is their parcel.
3. Those are their maps.
4. That's Tim's coffee.
5. Those are my clothes.
6. This is Pam's money.

4. *Example:*
Charlie / car (has got / motorbike)
— I'm sure that's Charlie's car.
— It can't be his. He's got a motorbike.

1. Mr Carter / office (work / surgery)
2. Mike and Jenny / house (live / flat)
3. your glasses (not wear / glasses)
4. Sergeant Salt / boat (not like / the sea)
5. Miss Smart / dog (has got / cat)
6. Uncle Bob / cigarettes (has got / pipe)

Summary of grammar

Possessive pronouns

Whose case is it?	**It's**	**mine.** **yours.** **his.** **hers.** **ours.** **yours.** **theirs.**	**It's**	**Bob's.** **the Inspector's.**

Verb + direct object + indirect object

Give	**it**	**to**	**me.** **him, her.** **Constable Potter.**
Show	**them**		**us.** **them.** **Mr and Mrs Carter.**

15

Notes de grammaire

1. **It's my case.** C'est ma valise.
   It's mine. C'est la mienne.
   Your case is over there. Votre valise est là-bas.
   Yours is over there. La vôtre est là-bas.

   They're my cases. Ce sont mes valises.
   They're mine. Ce sont les miennes.
   Your cases are over there. Vos valises sont là-bas.
   Yours are over there. Les vôtres sont là-bas.

En anglais, les pronoms possessifs (mine, his, yours, etc.) sont invariables.

2. **Give Pam a ticket.** Donne un billet à Pam.
   Give her a ticket. Donne-lui un billet.
   Give it to Pam. Donne-le à Pam.
   Give it to her. Donne-le lui.

Quand le complément d'objet direct est un pronom (it), le complément d'attribution (Pam / her) se place après le complément d'objet direct et est précédé de « to ».

3. **Whose sandwich is it?** A qui est le sandwich?
   Whose is it? A qui est-il?

« Whose » peut être adjectif ou pronom.

Vocabulaire

booking clerk employé au guichet (qui vend des billets)
case valise
cat chat
cheese fromage
inspector inspecteur
lost property objets trouvés
nightdress chemise de nuit
porter porteur
return ticket billet aller-retour
stomach estomac
word mot

silly idiot / bête

perhaps peut-être

if si

to buy acheter
to call appeler
to exist exister
to run courir
to show montrer
to stop arrêter / s'arrêter
to telephone téléphoner

I'm hungry J'ai faim
I'm sure. Je suis sûr.
It isn't anyone's. Il n'est à personne.
Il n'appartient à personne.

Exercises

1. *Example:*
you / go / supermarket / this afternoon
— Are you going to the supermarket this afternoon?
— Yes, I am. Can you give me a lift, please?

1. she / have lunch / with her uncle / tomorrow
2. you / visit / Mr Newton / at the weekend
3. Mike / go / doctor's / next Saturday
4. they / go / cinema / this evening
5. she / take her cat / vet's / on Monday
6. you and Pam / walk / town centre / this morning

2. *Example:*
anyone / the office
— Is there anyone in the office?
— Yes, of course there's someone in the office.

1. anything / the fridge
2. anyone / the front row
3. anything / that box
4. anyone / the classroom
5. anything / in your diary
6. anyone / in the shop

3. *Put a sentence from « A » with a sentence from « B », then complete the sentence with « must » or « mustn't ».*

A.
1. It's a great film.
2. Mr Carter's busy.
3. It's Dave's birthday tomorrow.
4. You're ill.
5. You're taking an exam tomorrow.
6. It's very cold.

B.
1. We ... buy him something.
2. You ... go to the doctor's.
3. You ... go to bed early.
4. You ... miss it.
5. You ... wear a coat.
6. You ... go into the surgery.

Summary of grammar

« Present continuous » with future meaning

What are you doing	tomorrow? on Friday? next week?

I'm going to the cinema	tomorrow. on Friday. next week.

« Must »

What must	I you he we you they	do?

I You He We You They	must	come. be quiet.

I You He We You They	mustn't	go. talk.

Contraction

mustn't	must not

Notes de grammaire

1. **He's getting up early tomorrow.** Il se lève de bonne heure demain.

Le présent progressif peut exprimer le futur.

2. **You must see it.** Il faut que tu le voies./Tu dois le voir.
   You mustn't miss it. Il ne faut pas que tu le manques./Tu ne dois pas le manquer.

« Must », comme « can », est suivi de l'infinitif sans « to ».

Notez les « question-tags » et les « short answers » de « must ».

You must go, mustn't you? Yes, I must.
He mustn't go, must he? No, he mustn't.

3. **I'm making something.**
   I'm not making anything.
   Are you making anything?

Les composés de « some » (someone, something) et « any » (anyone, anything) suivent les mêmes règles que « some » et « any » (voir chapitre 11).

4. **At Jenny's.** Chez Jenny.
   At the doctor's. Chez le médecin.

Notez la traduction de « chez » en anglais.

5. **Attention à l'orthographe : « another » s'écrit en un seul mot.**

Vocabulaire

America Amérique (États-Unis)
autobiography autobiographie
boxing match match de boxe
diary agenda
end fin
Member of Parliament député
something quelque chose
week semaine

another un(e) autre
busy occupé
great formidable/merveilleux
free libre
mad fou
next prochain

early tôt/de bonne heure
tomorrow demain

to fight se battre
to forget oublier
to go shopping faire les courses
to know (someone) connaître (quelqu'un)
to miss manquer
to take an exam passer un examen

I must... Il faut que je.../Je dois...
at the doctor's chez le médecin

17

Exercises

1. *Make six true sentences.*
Example:
London / big / Brighton
London's bigger than Brighton

London	old	cars
Pam	big	a chair
a bed	comfortable	buses
shoes	fast	socks
planes	expensive	Dave
Charlie	tall	Brighton
trains	quick	Rosie

2. *Example:*
thin cat
— Good heavens! What a thin cat!
— Yes, it's a lot thinner than ours.

1. heavy case
2. long ladder
3. good referee
4. big boot
5. intelligent dog
6. small office

3. *Example:*
Pam / tall / me
— What's Pam like?
— She's quite tall, but she isn't as tall as me.

1. the French teacher / friendly / Mike Carter
2. Jack's car / nice / Mike and Jenny
3. weather / windy / yesterday
4. that book / good / the film
5. your neighbour / nice / me
6. the new inspector / fat / Sergeant Salt

4. *Complete these sentences.*
1. How old ... you, Miss Smart?
2. It ... very hot today, ... it?
3. I think Sergeant Salt and Constable Potter ... silly.
4. What ... he like? He ... ... grey hair and he ... quite short.
5. What ... the weather like? It ... foggy.
6. «... you hungry?» «Yes, I ... .»

Summary of grammar

Comparatives

Joe's strong. **Sam isn't as strong as Joe.** **Joe's stronger than Sam.**
Sam's intelligent. **Joe isn't as intelligent as Sam.** **Sam's more intelligent than Joe.**

17

Notes de grammaire

1. **Is Sam as strong as Joe?** Est-ce que Sam est aussi fort que Joe?
   Yes, he's stronger than Joe, and he's more intelligent than Joe.
   Oui, il est plus fort que Joe, et il est plus intelligent que Joe.

Pour former le comparatif de supériorité (stronger, more intelligent), on ajoute la terminaison « -er » aux adjectifs courts, et « more » devant les adjectifs de trois syllabes ou plus.

2. **Good, better.** Bon, meilleur.
   Bad, worse. Mauvais, pire.

Notez les comparatifs irréguliers de « good » et « bad ».

3. **Attention à l'orthographe :**

   Big; bigger.
   Easy; easier.
   Heavy; heavier.

4. **They're outside.** Ils sont dehors.
   They're outside Mike's flat. Ils sont devant l'appartement de Mike.

Notez les deux emplois de « outside », qui peut être adverbe et préposition.

Vocabulaire

boot (of a car) coffre
boxer boxeur
fight rencontre (de boxe), match de boxe
ladder échelle
neighbour voisin
referee arbitre
seat place
winner gagnant

better meilleur
comfortable confortable
high haut
persuasive persuasif
quick rapide
second second / deuxième
wonderful merveilleux

nearly presque
together ensemble

to count compter
to park (se) garer
to serve servir
to start commencer
to use utiliser / se servir de
to worry s'inquiéter

all right d'accord
How old are you? Quel âge as-tu / avez-vous?
How tall are you? Combien mesures-tu / mesurez-vous?
in fact en fait
in the same way de la même façon
Ladies and gentlemen! Mesdames, messieurs!

18

Exercises

1. *Example:*
When / Mum / cover that chair
When's Mum going to cover that chair?

1. What / the inspector / do with that report
2. When / Uncle Bob / finish his boat
3. Who / you / telephone
4. Why / the manager / close the factory
5. How / you / sell that old car
6. Where / we / put our bicycles

2. *Example:*
you / watch the boxing match (Yes)
— Are you going to watch the boxing match?
— Yes, I am.

1. the referee / call the police (No)
2. she / give you some furniture (Yes)
3. Jack / live in America (Yes)
4. Mr Hardy / win the race (No)
5. the agent / sell another house (Yes)
6. the manager / give you a higher salary (No)

3. *Example:*
you / eat those sandwiches
— You musn't eat those sandwiches.
— Don't worry. I'm not going to eat them.

1. she / paint the front door
2. he / tell the teachers about the fire
3. you / forget me
4. they / start the fight
5. she / serve that woman
6. he / drop those cups

4. *Example:*
I / coat
I like that coat. I'm going to try it on.

1. Pam / shoes
2. Charlie / hat
3. Miss Smart / raincoat
4. Uncle Bob / trousers
5. Tim and Tony / boots
6. I / pullover

Summary of grammar

Future: « going to »

I'm You're He's We're You're They're	going to start.

I'm not You aren't He isn't We aren't You aren't They aren't	going to start.

Am I Are you Is he Are we Are you Are they	going to start?

Yes,	I am. you are. he is. we are. you are. they are.

No,	I'm not. you aren't. he isn't. we aren't. you aren't. they aren't.

He's going to start, isn't he? He isn't going to start, is he?
They're going to start, aren't they? They aren't going to start, are they?

Notes de grammaire

1. **Look! He's going to win!** Regarde! Il va gagner!

« Going to » exprime un futur proche.

I'm going to give him a guitar. Je vais lui donner une guitare.

On emploie aussi « going to » quand il s'agit d'une décision préméditée qu'on a la ferme intention d'exécuter (dans un avenir proche ou lointain).

2. **He's going to try the sunglasses on.**
He's going to try on the sunglasses. } Il va essayer les lunettes de soleil.

Remarquez la place de « on ». Le sens de la phrase ne change pas.

He's going to try them on. Il va les essayer.

Quand le complément est un pronom, « on » doit toujours être placé après ce pronom.

3. **He's got something in his hand.** Il a quelque chose à la main.

En anglais, les noms des parties du corps sont précédés de l'adjectif possessif, et non pas de l'article défini comme c'est souvent le cas en français.

4. **Attention à l'orthographe :**

A salary; two salaries.
A lady; two ladies.

Vocabulaire

bicycle bicyclette
employee employé
furniture meubles
hammer marteau
hand main
lady dame
manager directeur
meat viande
month mois
salary salaire
wall mur

low bas
young jeune

towards vers

to cover couvrir
to cut couper
to mean vouloir dire
to paint peindre
to put mettre
to sell vendre
to tell (someone) dire (à quelqu'un)
to try on essayer (un vêtement)

at the moment en ce moment
Pardon? Comment? / Pardon?
six days a week six jours par semaine

Exercises

1. *Example:*
the waiter / be happy in his new job (Yes)
— Will the waiter be happy in his new job?
— Yes, of course he will.

1. Mike and Jenny / give me a lift (Yes)
2. Brighton / be smaller in fifty years (No)
3. Arthur / like these bones (Yes)
4. The sky / be green in a thousand years (No)
5. you / write to me every week (Yes)
6. Tim and Tony / tell the headmaster (No)

2. *Example:*
Mr Newton / try to come next week
Mr Newton'll try to come next week, won't he?

1. Tim and Tony / be at school tomorrow
2. Mrs Carter / not burn her hand on the fire
3. I / miss the bus
4. You and Dave / not arrive late
5. That taxi driver / not take us to the airport
6. The sports teacher / want a hot bath

3. *Example:*
you / the hotel / be full (sleep in the car)
— What will you do if the hotel's full?
— I'll sleep in the car.

1. she / the weather / be bad (stay here)
2. he / the bus / not come (walk home)
3. you / the chicken / look bad (have steak and chips)
4. you / the doctor / not be free (wait for him)
5. you / he / park his car there (move it)
6. they / the plane / be late (go by train)

4. *Example:*
Miss Smart / nice
Miss Smart looks nice, doesn't she?

1. Uncle Bob / ill
2. Dave / stupid
3. Pam / great
4. Mrs Carter / quite young
5. this exercise / easy
6. those seats / comfortable

Summary of grammar

Future: « will »

I'll You'll He'll We'll You'll They'll	be early.

I You He We You They	won't be late.

Will	I you he we you they	be early?

Yes,	I will. you will. he will. we will. you will. they will.

No,	I won't you won't. he won't. we won't. you won't. they wont.

He'll be early, won't he? He won't be early, will he?

Contractions

He'll	He will
He won't	He will not

19

Notes de grammaire

1. **Sit down! You'll fall!** Assieds-toi! Tu vas tomber.
   It'll be a great photo. Ce sera une photo formidable.

« Will » exprime un futur inévitable, qui n'est pas le résultat d'une décision préméditée.

2. **I'll have steak and chips.** Je prendrai un steak frites.

Notez que « have » a ici le sens du verbe français « prendre ».

3. **Attention à l'orthographe :**
   A branch; two branches.

Vocabulaire

bread pain
branch branche
chips frites
country campagne
(a) hundred cent
lunch-time l'heure du déjeuner
soup potage
waiter garçon de café / serveur
world monde

stupid bête
vegetarian végétarien

probably probablement

to break casser
to fall tomber
to leave laisser
to need avoir besoin
to sit down s'asseoir
to slow down ralentir
to smoke fumer
to stand up se lever / se mettre debout

I'll look stupid. J'aurai l'air bête.
No smoking. Défense de fumer.

Exercises

1. *Example:*
Where / take this wallet / to the police station
— Where shall we take this wallet?
— Let's take it to the police station.

1. What / give Mum for her birthday / a book about Italy
2. What time / see Mike and Jenny tomorrow / about four
3. Where / put this picture / in the living-room
4. What colour / paint the kitchen / yellow
5. When / invite Tim and Tony to lunch / next Saturday
6. How much / give the waiter / twenty-five pence

2. *Example:*
He isn't very well. (stay in bed)
He isn't very well, is he? Why doesn't he stay in bed?

1. They can't see very well. (stand up)
2. Our car's ready now. (drive to the country)
3. There's a police car behind him. (slow down)
4. Our cases are heavy. (leave them at the station)
5. She doesn't need all that furniture. (sell it)
6. The politician isn't very good. (sit down)

3. *Example:*
We haven't got any money. (Charlie / give us some)
— Oh dear, we haven't got any money. What shall we do?
— Don't worry! Charlie'll give us some.

1. There aren't any matches. (I / buy a box)
2. The tyre's flat. (I / change the wheel)
3. We don't need all this junk. (we / burn it)
4. There aren't any trains to London today. (we / go by car)
5. There isn't any washing-powder. (I / buy a new packet)
6. I can't do this. (Charlie / help us)

4. *Example:*
walk to the river / an hour
— How long will it take to walk to the river?
— I'm not sure. About an hour, I think.

1. walk to the beach / ten minutes
2. drive round Brighton / half an hour
3. sail to France / twelve hours
4. finish this book / ten weeks
5. paint that furniture / two days
6. show him the house / twenty minutes

Summary of grammar

« Shall . . . »

What shall	**I**	**do?**
	we	

Why don't you leave?
Let's leave.

20

Notes de grammaire

1. **What shall we do?** Qu'allons-nous faire?
   Shall I tell him? Si je lui disais?

A la forme interrogative, « shall » à la première personne du singulier (« I ») et du pluriel (« we ») indique qu'on cherche à savoir l'avis des autres.

Shall we go to the cinema? Si nous allions au cinéma?
Let's go to the cinema. Allons au cinéma.
Why don't we go to the cinema? Pourquoi n'allons-nous pas au cinéma?

« Shall ..., let's ..., why don't ...? » expriment une suggestion.

2. **About five years.** Cinq ans environ.
   Think about it. Pensez-y.
   Tell me about Australia. Parlez-moi de l'Australie.

Notez les différents sens de « about ».

3. **She's right.** Elle a raison.
   He's hungry. Il a faim.
   I'm fourteen. J'ai quatorze ans.
   They're hot. Ils ont chaud.
   I'm cold. J'ai froid.

Attention à la traduction de « to be ».

4. **The news is good.** Les nouvelles sont bonnes.

Malgré sa forme pluriel, « news » s'emploie avec un verbe au singulier.

5. **Attention à l'orthographe :**

I catch; he catches.
A wish; two wishes.

Vocabulaire

Australia Australie
beginning début / commencement
daughter fille
farm ferme
help aide
hour heure
idea idée
news nouvelles
packet paquet
river fleuve / rivière
sailor marin
summer été
tyre pneu
(flat tyre pneu crevé**)**
washing lessive
washing-powder poudre à laver
wheel roue
winter hiver

about (eight months) environ (huit mois)

to catch (a bus) prendre (un autobus)
to leave partir
to sail naviguer / faire de la voile

Best wishes... Meilleurs vœux...
five and a half hours cinq heures et demie
How long? Combien de temps?
It'll only take a minute. Cela ne prendra qu'une minute.
She's right. Elle a raison.
Why don't you go to the cinema? Pourquoi ne vas-tu pas au cinéma?

21

Exercises

1. *Example:*
cup / on the floor
— Which cup's yours?
— The one on the floor.

1. lighter / on the desk
2. bicycle / between the car and the motorbike
3. jeans / in the washing-machine
4. letters / under the box
5. watch / on the table
6. seats / in the front row

2. *Example:*
Mrs Carter's ring / gold
— Which is Mrs Carter's ring?
— The gold one.

1. Dave's socks / yellow and red
2. Sergeant Salt's report / first
3. your cats / fat
4. Pam's watch / silver
5. your daughter's case / big black
6. Charlie's lighter / green plastic

3. *Complete these sentences with « which » or « what ».*

1. ... coat is yours?
2. ... time is it, please?
3. ... does « autobiography » mean?
4. ... are their names? Does anyone know?
5. ... bus do you catch, the 49 or the 82?
6. ... one do you like? The gold one or the silver one?

4. *Example:*
He wants to know the way to the station.
Can you tell him the way to the station, please?

1. I want to know the way to the swimming-pool.
2. Tony wants to know the way to the souvenir shop.
3. The sailors want to know the way to the pub.
4. We want to know the way to the square.
5. Pam wants to know the way to the post office.
6. My daughter wants to know the way to Mr Brown's farm.

Summary of grammar

« Which... ? » ; « the one, ones »

Which	**one** **lighter**	**do you like?**
	ones **lighters**	

I like the	**silver one.** **one on the shelf.**
	silver ones. **ones on the shelf.**

I like	**this one.** **that one.**

21

Notes de grammaire

1. **Which lighter do you like?** Quel est le briquet qui vous plaît?
   Which is your lighter? Lequel est votre briquet?

On emploie « which » (adjectif interrogatif ou pronom interrogatif) quand il s'agit d'un choix.

2. **My lighter's the blue one.** Mon briquet est celui qui est bleu.
   The ones on the shelf. Ceux qui sont sur l'étagère.

Le pronom « one » est employé pour éviter la répétition d'un nom. Il prend un « s » au pluriel.

3. **I like this one.**
   I don't like that one.
   I like these.
   I don't like those.

Notez qu'on n'emploie pas « ones » après les démonstratifs « these, those ».

4. **« We are very pleased to tell you... »**

Notez que dans une lettre officielle on n'emploie pas de « contractions ».

5. **I need some jeans.** J'ai besoin d'un « jean ».

Notez que « jeans » (comme « trousers ») n'existe qu'au pluriel.

Vocabulaire

cheque chèque
girl fille
lighter briquet
present cadeau
post office bureau de poste
record-player tourne-disque
shop assistant vendeur (vendeuse)
square place
ring bague
watch montre

gold en or
plastic en matière plastique
pleased content
silver en argent

then puis
between entre

to act jouer (un rôle)
to collect ramasser / cueillir

Can you tell me the way? Pourriez-vous m'indiquer le chemin?
Congratulations! Félicitations!
on the left à gauche
on the right à droite

Page 100

milk lait

Chanson : page 103

smoke fumée
sun soleil

to hold tenir

Revision exercises 4

Exercise 1

Example:
bike / Rosie
Hey, don't take that bike! It's Rosie's.

1. shoes / Dave
2. ladder / Mr Kipper
3. trousers / Pam
4. seat / Mr Newton
5. case / Miss Smart
6. fish / the cat

Exercise 2

Answer these questions. Make true sentences about yourself.

1. Do you like cheese?
2. Do you drink a lot of milk?
3. How old are you?
4. What are you like? Have you got long or short hair? Are you quite tall or quite short?
5. Are you going to take any exams this year?
6. Have you got a cat?
7. Are you going shopping on Saturday?
8. Do you often miss the bus?
9. Do you know any English people?
10. How many books are there in your bag?
11. Have you got a diary? Do you write in it every day?
12. Can you count to a hundred in English?

Exercise 3

Example:
Is your car bigger than Jack's?
Of course it isn't. Mine isn't nearly as big as Jack's.

1. Is your flat nicer than Jack's?
2. Is your car more comfortable than Jack's?
3. Is your bike faster than Jack's?
4. Are your records better than Jack's?
5. Is your salary higher than Jack's?
6. Are your shirts whiter than Jack's?
7. Are your clothes more expensive than Jack's?
8. Are your friends sillier than Jack's?

Exercise 4

Example:
Pam / tomorrow / go to the cinema
— What's Pam doing tomorrow?
— She's going to the cinema.

1. Rosie / this afternoon / wash her hair
2. Dave / on Saturday / go to a football match
3. Mr and Mrs Carter / this evening / go out to dinner
4. Sam Sly / next week / fight Joe Bix
5. Dave / tomorrow / take an exam
6. Mike and Jenny / at the weekend / paint their living-room
7. Uncle Bob / next year / sail to Australia
8. Miss Smart / on Saturday night / have dinner in a Chinese restaurant

Exercise 5

Complete these sentences with "can, can't, must", and "mustn't".

1. You ... park here. That notice says "No parking."
2. I ... see anything. Where's the light switch?
3. We need more money. We ... make more clothes.
4. You ... have it. I don't want it.
5. I ... talk to you now. I'm too busy.
6. You ... smoke. It's making you ill.

Exercise 6

Can you complete these sentences?

1. You're going too fast. Slow ...!
2. When Mr Hardy comes into the classroom, everyone stands ... .
3. What are you doing in that tree? Come ...!
4. Please stop the car. I want to get ... .
5. Good morning, Miss Brown. Come ... . Sit ... .
6. What are they all waiting ...?
7. What time do you usually get ...?
8. They're listening ... their instructions.
9. Pam's looking ... a job, isn't she?
10. Can I try these sunglasses ..., please?
11. Of course I'll give you a lift. Get ... .
12. Does Pam often go ... in the evening?

Exercise 7

Example:
That's my scarf.
— Whose scarf is that?
— It's mine. Give it to me.

1. That's my case.
2. Those are his glasses.
3. That's her diary.
4. Those are our chips.
5. Those are their toothbrushes.
6. That's my soup.

Exercise 8

Put these words into the plural, and then write sentences with the words.

Example:
policeman
There are ten policemen in our classroom.

1. fireman
2. tooth
3. salary
4. branch
5. lady
6. tomato
7. woman
8. bus
9. watch
10. nightdress
11. box
12. air-hostess

Revision exercises 4

Exercise 9

Example:
you / do anything tomorrow
You aren't doing anything tomorrow, are you?

1. she / see anyone this evening
2. you / cook anything for dinner
3. they / give him anything for his birthday
4. he / go out with anyone on Saturday
5. we / buy anything at the supermarket
6. you / give anyone a lift this evening

Exercise 10

Example:
trousers
— These trousers are great, aren't they?
— Yes, I'm going to try them on.

1. shoes
2. red shirt
3. sunglasses
4. plastic raincoat
5. long skirt
6. jeans
7. hat
8. yellow boots
9. pink bikini
10. black pullover

Exercise 11

Example:
have for lunch / steak and chips
— What shall we have for lunch?
— I know! We'll have steak and chips.

1. have for dinner / fish and chips
2. do this evening / go to the swimming-pool
3. tell Mr Hardy / tell him we're ill
4. show the inspector / show him some old tickets
5. do at the weekend / paint the bedroom
6. cook for lunch / make a chicken pie

Exercise 12

Example:
drop this cup / it / break
— What'll happen if I drop this cup?
— It'll break, of course!

1. fight Joe Bix / he / win
2. walk along that rope / you / fall
3. taste this hot soup / you / burn your tongue
4. ask Charlie to help me / he / say yes
5. stand on that branch / it / break
6. wear a pink bikini at school / everyone / think you're mad

Exercise 13

Example:
coat / brown

A: Can you give me my coat, please?
B: Of course. Which one is it?
A: It's the brown one.
B: Here you are.

1. scarf / long white
2. hat / on the top shelf
3. jeans / on the floor
4. lighter / blue plastic
5. socks / green and red
6. keys / under that wallet

Exercise 14

Write these sentences again, with contractions.

Example:
I will see you tomorrow then.
I'll see you tomorrow then.

1. I do not think he will like the vegetarian restaurant.
2. Hurry up! We will miss the bus.
3. Do not worry! It will not take long.
4. She is going to buy a packet of "Ozo" washing-powder.
5. You must not do that. It is a stupid idea.
6. They are going to sell all their furniture.

22

Exercises

1. *Example:*
food in the fridge (Yes)
— Is there much food in the fridge?
— Yes, there's a lot of food in the fridge.

1. furniture in the flat (Yes)
2. employees at the factory (No)
3. bread in the kitchen (No)
4. washing-powder in the packet (Yes)
5. girls at your school (Yes)
6. eggs in the box (No)

2. *Complete the sentences with «much, many» or «a lot»:*

1. That English girl doesn't speak ... French.
2. There's ... to do in Brighton, isn't there?
3. Waiter! We haven't got ... potatoes!
4. I mustn't eat ... at dinner-time.
5. There isn't ... room in this office, is there?
6. I'm sure they won't collect ... money.
7. I can't see ... people in the sea.
8. There isn't ... news in the newspaper today.
9. That boy isn't talking ..., is he?
10. Will there be ... to eat at Jack's party?
11. Have we got ... plates, Uncle Bob?
12. We'll need ... of cushions, you know.

3. *Example:*
you / chicken pie
— Do you want any chicken pie?
— Oh, no chicken pie for me! I'm getting too fat!

1. he / ice-cream
2. Arthur / a sausage
3. she / a piece of toast
4. you / sugar in your tea
5. they / sandwiches
6. you and Mike / fish and chips

Summary of grammar

«Much, many, a lot of»

Is	**there**	**much**	**butter?**
Are		**many**	**eggs?**

Yes, there	**is**	**a lot of**	**butter.**
	are		**eggs.**

No, there	**isn't**	**much**	**butter.**
	aren't	**many**	**eggs.**

Notes de grammaire

1. **Is there much food?** Y a-t-il beaucoup de nourriture?
   No, there isn't much food. Non, il n'y a pas beaucoup de nourriture.
   Are there many plates? Y a-t-il beaucoup d'assiettes?
   No, there aren't many plates. Non, il n'y a pas beaucoup d'assiettes.

Dans les phrases interrogatives et négatives, on emploie « much » devant les noms indénombrables, et « many » devant les noms pluriels.

There's a lot of food. Il y a beaucoup de nourriture.
There are a lot of plates. Il y a beaucoup d'assiettes.

On emploie « a lot of » dans les phrases affirmatives, devant les indénombrables et devant les noms pluriels.

Is there a lot of food?
There aren't a lot of plates.

« A lot of » peut aussi remplacer « much, many » dans les phrases interrogatives et négatives.

2. **There isn't much.**
   We haven't got many.
   I've got a lot.

« Much, many, a lot » peuvent être pronoms.

3. **There isn't much room.** Il n'y a pas beaucoup de place.
   There aren't many rooms. Il n'y a pas beaucoup de chambres.

Attention aux deux sens de « room » en anglais.

4. **No sausages for me.** Pas de saucisses pour moi.
   No sugar for me. Pas de sucre pour moi.
   No parking. Stationnement interdit.

Remarquez le sens de « no », adjectif.

5. **Attention à l'orthographe :**

   A potato; two potatoes.
   A glass; two glasses.

Vocabulaire

camping-gas camping-gaz
cushion coussin
drink boisson
egg œuf
glass verre
lump (of sugar) morceau (de sucre)
piece morceau
plate assiette
potato pomme de terre
sausage saucisse

delicious délicieux

to fill remplir
to get cold se refroidir
to get fat grossir

Just one. Un(e) seul(e)/Juste un(e).
There isn't much room. Il n'y a pas beaucoup de place.
What's the matter with them? Qu'est-ce qu'ils ont?

Exercises

1. *Example:*
Mike's car / at the garage / yesterday (Yes)
— Was Mike's car at the garage yesterday?
— Yes, it was.

1. the flats in Park Street / for sale / last week (No)
2. you / at the party / on Saturday (No)
3. Arthur / in the cupboard / this morning (Yes)
4. camping-gas / in Charlie's tent / last night (Yes)
5. the actors / ready / at half past seven (Yes)
6. you and Dave / in the post office / this afternoon (Yes)

2. *Example:*
the film / very good
— What was the film like?
— It was very good.

1. the sausages / not very big
2. your holiday / great
3. people in the hotel / not very friendly
4. the storm / incredible
5. the photos / not very good
6. his boat / white with red sails

3. *Example:*
a policeman in the manager's office
— There was a policeman in the manager's office, wasn't there?
— Yes, there was.

1. a lot of people on the river yesterday
2. a terrible noise at the football match
3. six dogs in the surgery this morning
4. a lot of things at the Lost Property Office
5. an enormous plane at the airport yesterday
6. a lot of room in Mr Hardy's new boat

4. *Example:*
she / asleep
She's asleep, isn't she?

1. they / asleep
2. he / awake
3. they / frightened
4. you / tired
5. she / hungry
6. they / right

Summary of grammar

Simple past: « to be »

Where	was I were you was he were we were you were they	yesterday?

I was You were He was We were You were They were	at home yesterday.

He was at home yesterday, wasn't he? He wasn't at home yesterday, was he?	Yes, he was. No, he wasn't.
They were at home yesterday, weren't they? They weren't at home yesterday, were they?	Yes, they were. No, they weren't.

Contractions

wasn't	was not
weren't	were not

Notes de grammaire

1. **He's asleep.** Il dort.
   He's sleeping at the hotel tonight. Il dort à l'hôtel ce soir.

En anglais, on dit « he's asleep » et non « he's sleeping » quand il s'agit simplement de l'état de sommeil.

2. **He's much smaller than Joe.**
   He's a lot smaller than Joe. } Il est beaucoup plus petit que Joe.

On emploie « much » ou « a lot » comme adverbe devant le comparatif.

3. **They're getting heavier and heavier.** Elles deviennent de plus en plus lourdes.
   It's getting more and more interesting. Cela devient de plus en plus intéressant.

Notez la traduction de « plus en plus ».

Vocabulaire

actor acteur / comédien
blanket couverture
cupboard placard
dream rêve
storm orage

awful affreux
tired fatigué

to be frightened avoir peur
to dream rêver
to remember se rappeler / se souvenir de

He's asleep. Il dort / Il est endormi
He's awake. Il est réveillé.
Five miles from the beach. A cinq miles de la plage.

Exercises

1. *Example:*
Bob and Patrick / decide to go to Australia (last week)
— When did Bob and Patrick decide to go to Australia?
— They decided to go to Australia last week.

1. Uncle Bob / shout at Patrick (last night)
2. Pam / invite you to her party (on Sunday)
3. Miss Smart / offer Pam a job (last Monday)
4. Mr Carter / cook his breakfast (at seven thirty)
5. The actor / jump out of the window (yesterday)
6. Mr Newton / open the new supermarket (on Saturday)

2. *Example:*
— Did you invite Patrick?
— No, I didn't. I invited Miss Smart.

1. Did he dance with Pam?
2. Did they wait for Mike?
3. Did she talk to Jenny?
4. Did you show it to Dave?
5. Did you want to see Charlie?
6. Did they stop at Bob's house?

3. *Complete these sentences with: « delicious, interesting, funny, thin, nice, strong ».*

1. « Why is he laughing? » « He's reading something ... . »
2. Did you talk to anyone ...?
3. What shall I wear? I haven't got anything ... .
4. It's very heavy. Ask someone ... .
5. I'm going to cook something ... .
6. These jeans are too small for me. I'll give them to someone ... .

4. *Give the short answers to these questions.*

1. Did Bob have a beard when he was young? No, ...
2. Was Charlie very miserable? Yes, ...
3. Is your raincoat dry now? No, ...
4. Were there many people at the party? No, ...
5. Did Pam and Rosie drink all the whisky? Yes, ...
6. Was the bottle really empty? Yes, ...

Summary of grammar

Simple past: regular verbs

I You He We You They	finished it yesterday.

Did	I you he we you they	finish it yesterday?

Yes,	I you he we you they	did.

No,	I you he we you they	didn't.

He finished it yesterday, didn't he? He didn't finish it yesterday, did he?

Contraction

didn't	did not

Notes de grammaire

1. He listened and waited.

On forme le prétérit (« simple past ») des verbes réguliers en ajoutant « -ed » à l'infinitif.

He decided to stay.
He invited us to his party.

Si l'infinitif se termine par « -e », on ajoute simplement « -d ».

Attention à la prononciation!
Le suffixe « -ed » se prononce de trois façons différentes :

a) **rained, listened, happened, opened, showed, offered [d].**
b) **stopped, cooked, looked, walked, talked, danced, laughed, jumped [t].**
c) **decided, waited, shouted, wanted, invited [id].**

2. Did you meet anyone interesting? As-tu rencontré quelqu'un d'intéressant?
She wanted something funny. Elle voulait quelque chose de drôle.

En anglais, l'adjectif se place tout de suite après « anyone, something, someone, etc. ».

Vocabulaire

beard barbe
bottle bouteille
gate barrière
lesson leçon

dry sec
empty vide
funny drôle / bizarre
miserable malheureux

to laugh rire
to shout crier

for six hours pendant six heures

Exercises

1. *Answer these questions. Make true sentences about yourself.*

1. What time did you go to bed last night?
2. What did you think of the dialogue in this chapter?
3. What did you have for breakfast this morning?
4. What time did you come to school this morning?
5. What did you give your friend for his / her last birthday?
6. What time did you get up this morning?

2. *Complete these sentences with a verb in the « simple past ».*

1. Look! I ... this gold ring in the garden yesterday.
2. I can't find my English book. I think I ... it on the bus this morning.
3. He ... frightened because he ... an enormous, silver fish.
4. Dave ... some fantastic photos on the beach.
5. Mrs Carter ... some blankets in the sale.
6. He ... his cup on the table and ... to the front door.

3. *Example:*
milk / buy / two bottles
— How much milk did you buy?
— I bought two bottles.

1. sugar / have / four lumps
2. cushions / make / twelve
3. whisky / buy / three bottles
4. packets of washing-powder / give him / one
5. farms / visit / five
6. bread / take / two pieces

4. *Complete these sentences with a question-tag.*

1. The postman's at the door, ...
2. Rosie and Dave made an awful noise, ...
3. Miss Smart didn't dance with anyone, ...
4. We thought it was wonderful, ...
5. Sergeant Salt didn't go back to the police station, ...
6. The two Americans were very lucky, ...

Summary of grammar

Simple past: irregular verbs

Did you	**have ...?**	**come ...?**
	go ...?	**put ...?**
	get up ...?	**find ...?**
	make ...?	**think ...?**
	take ...?	**buy ...?**
	leave ...?	**give ...?**
	see ...?	**run ...?**

Yes, I	**had ...**	**came ...**
	went ...	**put ...**
	got up ...	**found ...**
	made ...	**thought ...**
	took ...	**bought ...**
	left ...	**gave ...**
	saw ...	**ran ...**

No, I didn't	**have ...**	**come ...**
	go ...	**put ...**
	get up ...	**find ...**
	make ...	**think ...**
	take ...	**buy ...**
	leave ...	**give ...**
	see ...	**run ...**

25

Notes de grammaire

1. **Did you go to the party?**
   No, I didn't go to the party.
   I went to the cinema.

Un grand nombre de verbes courants ont un prétérit (« simple past ») irrégulier. Mais la forme interrogative et négative du prétérit se construit de la même façon que celle des verbes réguliers, à l'aide de « did ».

2. **He went back to the shop.** Il est retourné au magasin.
   He went down the street. Il a descendu la rue.
   He went up the street. Il a remonté la rue.

En anglais, c'est souvent une préposition qui indique la direction du mouvement, et non pas un verbe comme en français.

Vocabulaire

double bed grand lit (pour deux personnes)
electric blanket couverture chauffante
postman facteur
sale soldes
single bed lit pour une personne

over au-dessus

too much trop

to be lucky avoir de la chance
to go back retourner

Exercises

1. *Complete these sentences with a reflexive pronoun.*

1. I didn't enjoy ... at your party, you know.
2. « He fell into an enormous hole. » « Good heavens! Did he hurt ... ? »
3. Miss Smart often looks at ... in the mirror.
4. I don't know why they came. They didn't enjoy ... .
5. It's great, isn't it? We made it ... .
6. Be careful! You'll cut ... .

2. *Example:*

— Did Mike help Rosie to make the table?
— No, he didn't. She made it herself.

1. Did Mrs Carter help Pam to find the job?
2. Did Mr Carter help his wife to paint the living-room?
3. Did Jenny help Mike to make the cupboard?
4. Did Sergeant Salt help you to find the park?
5. Did Miss Smart help Bob to serve the customers?
6. Did your friend help you to do this exercise?

3. *Read the passage, and then complete it.*

Pam usually ... work at nine o'clock. This morning she ... very late. She ... of bed and ... to the bathroom. But Dave ... in the bathroom. « Dave! I'm in a hurry, » she ... . « I'm ..., Pam, » ... Dave. « Don't worry! It'll only ... me a minute ». Pam ... very surprised because Dave didn't usually ... . But she ... to her bedroom and ... . Half an hour later, Dave ... of the bathroom. Pam ... n't very pleased, but when she ... Dave she ... . He ... very funny, because he ... elastoplast all over his face!

Now complete the passage with these verbs; be careful, put them into the correct tense.

to answer, to be (2), to come out, to get out, to go back, to have, to laugh, to look, to run, to see, to shave (2), to shout, to start, to take, to wait, to wake up.

Summary of grammar

Reflexive pronouns

I		**myself.**
You		**yourself.**
He		**himself.**
She	**enjoyed**	**herself.**
We		**ourselves.**
You		**yourselves.**
They		**themselves.**

Notes de grammaire

1. **I burnt myself.** Je me suis brûlé.
   He hurt himself. Il s'est fait mal.
   She cut herself. Elle s'est coupée.
   We enjoyed ourselves. Nous nous sommes bien amusés.

Les pronoms réfléchis (myself, himself, etc.) transforment le verbe en verbe pronominal.

N.B. **He got up.** Il s'est levé.
He washed. Il s'est lavé.
He shaved. Il s'est rasé.
He got dressed. Il s'est habillé.

En anglais, il y a très peu de verbes pronominaux.

2. **I did it myself.** Je l'ai fait moi-même.
   Do it yourself. Fais-le toi-même.

Les pronoms réfléchis renforcent le sujet.

3. **Attention à l'orthographe :**

   ... self; ... selves.
   A shelf; two shelves.
   To shave; he's shaving.

Irregular verbs :

To burn; I burnt.
To cut; I cut.
To fall; I fell.
To run; I ran.
To wake up; I woke up.
To hurt; I hurt.

Vocabulaire

« Do-it-yourself » bricolage
face visage
father père
mirror miroir
paint peinture
wallpaper papier peint

before avant

quickly vite / rapidement

to shave se raser
to wake up se réveiller

Goodbye
He enjoyed himself. Il s'est bien amusé.
He hurt himself. Il s'est fait mal.
I'm in a hurry. Je suis pressé.

Exercises

1. *Example:*
Charlie / have a cup of coffee
— What was Charlie doing?
— He was having a cup of coffee.

1. Uncle Bob / talk to Miss Smart
2. Dave and Rosie / look at the boats
3. Arthur / play in the garden
4. Mrs Carter / write a letter
5. Mr Carter / shave
6. you and Pam / smoke

2. *Look at the pictures on page 124 and answer these questions.*

1. At half past two, what were Dave and Rosie doing?
2. What was Mr Carter doing at three o'clock?
3. What was Mr Carter doing at half past three?
4. What were Dave and Rosie doing at four o'clock?
5. What do you think Dave and Rosie were doing at half past three?

3. *Look at the big picture at the top of the following pages:*

1. On page 14, what were Dave and Rosie doing?
2. On page 18, what was Uncle Bob doing?
3. On page 30, what were Mr Carter and Rosie doing?
4. On page 46, what was Pam doing?
5. On page 54, what was Mrs Carter doing?
6. On page 62, what was Mike doing? What was the weather like?
7. On page 74, what were the people at the station doing?
8. On page 86, what were the people in the chemist's shop doing?

4. *Example:*
Uncle Bob was enjoying himself.
— Uncle Bob was enjoying himself, wasn't he?
— Yes, he was.

1. Dave was dreaming.
2. Rosie wasn't listening.
3. Mrs Carter was playing the piano.
4. Bob was talking to a customer.
5. Mr and Mrs Carter weren't shouting.
6. Pam and Dave were getting cold.

Summary of grammar

Past continuous

I was	**dreaming.**
You were	
He was	
We were	
You were	
They were	

I wasn't	**dreaming.**
You weren't	
He wasn't	
We weren't	
You weren't	
They weren't	

Was I	**dreaming?**
Were you	
Was he	
Were we	
Were you	
Were they	

Yes,	**I was.**
	you were.
	he was.
	we were.
	you were.
	they were.

No,	**I wasn't.**
	you weren't.
	he wasn't.
	we weren't.
	you weren't.
	they weren't.

He was dreaming, wasn't he?
They weren't dreaming, were they?

27

Notes de grammaire

1. **They were listening to records.** Ils écoutaient des disques.

On emploie le prétérit progressif (« past continuous ») pour décrire une action en cours dans le passé. Le plus souvent, on ne sait pas quand cette action a commencé.

2. **I thought (that) Bob was going to sell it.** Je pensais que Bob allait le vendre.

Rappelez-vous qu'on supprime souvent la conjonction « that » après « to think », « to say » (voir chapitre 14).

3. **Have a cup of coffee!** Prends une tasse de café!
We had a good holiday. Nous avons passé de bonnes vacances.
Have a bath! Prends un bain!
He's having English lessons. Il suit des cours d'anglais.
Have a nice day! Bonne journée!

Notez les différentes traductions de « have ».

Vocabulaire

upset ennuyé / bouleversé

soon bientôt

We'll be all right. Ça ira.

28

Exercises

1. *Example:*
Uncle Bob took a scarf. I gave it to him.
Uncle Bob took the scarf I gave him.

1. He took some shoes. Charlie gave them to him.
2. Charlie was eating a chicken pie. Pam made it.
3. Bob was reading a letter. Patrick wrote it.
4. This is the race. Mr Hardy always wins it.
5. That's the girl. I talked to her.
6. I don't like the wallpaper. Mrs Carter bought it.

2. *Example:*
Don't take that book. Rosie's reading it.
Don't take that book. It's the one that Rosie's reading.

1. Ask that man. He sells the tickets.
2. Don't buy that skirt. Pam wants it.
3. Give Charlie some whisky. He looks upset.
4. Here's the postcard. Mrs Carter wrote it.
5. You mustn't use that cup. Mr Carter always uses it.
6. She can take my camera. It's in the cupboard.

3. *Complete these sentences with « who » or « that ».*

1. Do you know the woman ... painted that picture?
2. Uncle Bob's talking to the man ... sailed round the world last year.
3. He wanted a book ... was on the top shelf.
4. You can't wear shoes ... are full of holes!
5. Mr Hardy's the one ... works at Grove School.
6. Is this the milk ... was in the fridge?
7. You must catch the train ... leaves at half past nine.
8. Do you know many people ... live in Brighton?
9. At the moment, he's on a plane ... is going to New York.
10. I danced with a boy ... wanted to dance with Pam.
11. Uncle Bob doesn't like customers ... never buy anything.
12. I'm waiting for a bus ... goes to the swimming-pool.

Summary of grammar

Relative pronouns

This is the	**letter that** **girl who**	**came this morning.**

This is the	**letter** **girl**	**I saw this morning.**

28

Notes de grammaire

1. **Take** $\left.\begin{matrix}\textbf{the bag}\\ \textbf{the one}\end{matrix}\right\}$ **that isn't full of holes.** Prends $\left.\begin{matrix}\text{le sac}\\ \text{celui}\end{matrix}\right\}$ qui n'est pas plein de trous.

Le pronom relatif « that » s'emploie pour les choses, les animaux, (et pour les personnes aussi).

$\left.\begin{matrix}\textbf{The girl}\\ \textbf{The one}\end{matrix}\right\}$ **who sailed round the world.** $\left.\begin{matrix}\text{La fille}\\ \text{Celle}\end{matrix}\right\}$ qui a navigué autour du monde.

Le pronom relatif « who » ne s'emploie que pour les personnes.

2. **The bag (that) I gave you.** Le sac que je t'ai donné.
   The girl (that) we saw yesterday. La fille que nous avons vue hier.

Quand le pronom relatif est complément d'objet, il est le plus souvent sous-entendu.

Irregular verbs :

To win; I won.
To write; I wrote.

Vocabulaire

Good luck! Bonne chance!

Chanson : page 135

inside à l'intérieur

Two year Course • First Book

Imagine you're English

D. Gibbs
B. Sc. (Hons.) London
N. Goodey
B. A. (Hons.) London
Grad. Cert. in Education (Manchester)
F. Morel R. Thomas

avec la collaboration
d'H. Clément
Agrégée de l'Université

illustrations
de R. Blachon

Classe de 4e • Seconde langue

Formation permanente des adultes

Librairie Classique Eugène Belin - 8, rue Férou - 75278 Paris Cedex 06

Préface

Aux élèves

Notre but

Nous avons écrit ce livre pour vous qui abordez l'étude de l'anglais comme deuxième ou même troisième langue, c'est-à-dire pour de « grands débutants ».

Le but d'« Imagine you're English: Two-year course » est de vous donner une connaissance pratique de l'anglais, afin que vous puissiez comprendre et parler cette langue dans toutes sortes de situations quotidiennes. C'est aussi de vous parler de l'Angleterre et des Anglais.

Les personnages du livre

Dans le « First Book » vous ferez la connaissance de la famille Carter, qui habite Brighton, sur la côte Sud de l'Angleterre.

Pam Carter travaille dans une pharmacie ; son frère, Dave, est un passionné de photographie ; leur jeune sœur, Rosie, a l'art de mettre les gens mal à l'aise par un certain franc-parler...

Leur meilleur ami, Charlie, est mécanicien dans un garage. Il vit chez son oncle Bob, qui tient un magasin de brocante à Brighton et dont le passe-temps favori est la voile ; sa grande ambition : le tour du monde sur un voilier...

Vous verrez aussi Miss Smart, qui dirige un bureau d'embauche : son caractère paisible change du tout au tout dès qu'elle est au volant d'une voiture.

Enfin, il y a le « Sergeant Salt » et le « Constable Potter », dont les efforts pour maintenir la loi et l'ordre vous feront rire.

Votre rôle dans le livre

Si vous voulez vraiment réussir avec « Imagine you're English », il faut jouer vous-même un rôle important. Les personnages du livre forment un groupe très vivant : il leur arrive de se disputer, ils font des gestes, se déplacent... Nous voulons que vous les imitiez. A partir des situations dans lesquelles ils se trouvent, c'est à vous de créer : jouer vos propres situations et improviser vos propres dialogues.

Alors, n'oubliez pas : Levez-vous ! Parlez ! Bougez ! Si vous voulez parler anglais, il vous faut vivre en anglais.

Cassettes et disques

Nous vous proposons des cassettes et des disques pour vous permettre de rester à l'« écoute » d'Imagine you're English.

Sur les trois cassettes vous trouverez pour chaque chapitre :
— la première page ;
— le dialogue principal ;
— les chansons du livre, et les « drills » qui ne sont pas imprimés dans votre livre mais qui sont l'occasion d'une révision purement orale.

Sur les six disques vous pourrez entendre chez vous les dialogues de chaque chapitre et les 4 chansons.

Ces matériels constituent un répétiteur très efficace pour le travail individuel.

Bon courage !

ISBN 2-7011-0263-5

Aux professeurs

Imagine you're English: Two-year course

« Imagine you're English: Two-year course » a été conçu pour les élèves qui ont besoin d'acquérir en deux ans une **connaissance pratique de l'anglais.** Au bout de deux ans, après avoir étudié le First et le Second Book, les élèves auront à leur disposition un vocabulaire d'environ 1 500 mots et auront appris toutes les structures grammaticales indispensables à une bonne pratique de la langue.

Les caractéristiques essentielles du « First Book »

— **Des activités variées** figurent dans chaque chapitre. C'est un bon moyen de renouveler constamment l'intérêt d'une classe et cette variété, allant de pair avec la bonne humeur du livre, incitera les élèves à travailler avec plaisir... donc avec succès.

— **Les situations** du livre, tout autant que les dessins, permettent à l'élève de trouver le sens d'un texte : nous les avons choisies fortement typées et divertissantes. Plus une situation est frappante, mieux elle aide à fixer la langue dans la mémoire de l'élève.

— **Les structures nouvelles** sont enseignées de façon claire et systématique : les élèves doivent toujours savoir exactement ce qu'ils sont en train de faire. Toutefois, c'est quand les élèves s'essaient eux-mêmes à utiliser les structures qu'on peut vraiment juger de leurs capacités. Aussi leur avons-nous donné de multiples occasions d'appliquer et de pratiquer ce qu'ils apprennent : c'est par **une participation active** et un effort **d'imagination** que les élèves assimilent des connaissances.

Tout au long du livre, structure et vocabulaire sont **systématiquement réemployés.** Cette périodicité de la révision donne aux élèves une grande assurance ; elle permet aussi de progresser à **un rythme soutenu** qui maintient en éveil l'intérêt de la classe.

Les illustrations

La **clarté** des dessins de Roger Blachon permettra aux élèves de bien saisir le sens du texte. Par ailleurs, leur caractère **divertissant** aidera à le mémoriser et contribuera à créer dans la classe une atmosphère gaie et décontractée, favorable à **l'expression spontanée** des élèves. Le « cache » permet aux élèves de couvrir le texte pendant qu'ils regardent les illustrations et écoutent le professeur ou la bande magnétique.

Le livre : contenu

Chacun des 28 chapitres comporte 4 pages.

En 1re page, est exposé **le point de grammaire** sur lequel repose tout le chapitre. Chaque structure nouvelle est présentée dans une situation qui démontre clairement son utilisation et en donne de nombreux exemples.

En 2e page — sous la rubrique « Questions » — sont introduites **les formes interrogatives** qui correspondent aux structures de la première page. Une fois assimilés les exemples du livre, les élèves peuvent, sur le même modèle, construire leurs propres questions et donner les réponses.
Sous la rubrique « **Practice** », figurent différentes activités qui donnent l'occasion d'utiliser les structures nouvelles. Les élèves font des phrases d'après des dessins, parlent d'eux-mêmes, de leurs amis, de ce qui les intéresse ; ils créent de courts dialogues. Dans les derniers chapitres, cette page comporte des exercices de prononciation et d'orthographe.

Le dialogue de la 3e page met en pratique la nouvelle structure, d'une façon moins « concentrée » que la première page, et permet la révision du vocabulaire des chapitres précédents. Il introduit aussi un certain nombre **d'expressions idiomatiques** qui donneront à l'élève la possibilité de parler un anglais naturel et vivant.
Tous les dialogues sont courts et, après les avoir étudiés, des groupes d'élèves peuvent les **jouer.** Il ne s'agit pas de reproduire exactement le texte original mais de re-créer la situation : les élèves retiendront mieux les phrases qu'ils auront improvisées eux-mêmes. La dramatisation leur permet de s'exprimer totalement en anglais : par la parole, mais aussi par les gestes, les expressions du visage, tout comme dans n'importe quelle conversation.

La 4e page est tantôt une page de référence, tantôt un « Passage for comprehension ».

— **Les pages de référence** exploitent les registres de base du vocabulaire : nombres, temps, description des gens et des vêtements, noms de pays... Elles donnent aux élèves des outils pour un travail plus créatif.

— **Les « Passages for comprehension »** proposent une grande variété de textes : le commentaire d'un match de boxe, une carte postale, une lettre, une publicité, un article de journal... Ces textes ne comportent pas de grammaire nouvelle et quasiment pas de vocabulaire nouveau. D'une façon générale, ils ne sont pas illustrés : les élèves commencent à prendre confiance en eux-mêmes dès qu'ils arrivent à comprendre un texte sans aucun support visuel. Les « Passages for comprehension » peuvent être faits en classe ou à la maison. Dans le second cas, ce sera un bon entraînement à la lecture silencieuse.

La quatrième page comporte parfois un « Practice » supplémentaire.

Révision

Il y a, après les chapitres 5, 8, 14, 21 et 28, une « section de révision » à laquelle correspondent, dans le Triliber, des exercices qui peuvent servir de **tests de contrôle.**

Quatre chansons ont été intégrées dans la progression grammaticale et lexicale du livre. Chacune permet de réviser les structures et le vocabulaire appris jusqu'alors.

Le Triliber

Ce petit livret offre deux possibilités d'utilisation.

1. Triliber ouvert et livre ouvert.
Seule la page de gauche du Triliber est alors visible. C'est **une page de référence** en anglais et en français, comprenant des notes de grammaire et d'orthographe et une liste de mots anglais-français. Cette page est essentiellement destinée au travail personnel de l'élève à la maison : elle lui permet de rattraper sans difficultés des leçons manquées à cause d'une absence.

2. Triliber ouvert et livre fermé.
Sur la page de droite du Triliber, **une série d'exercices** et **un tableau de récapitulation** (« summary table ») du point de grammaire étudié dans le chapitre. Pendant que les élèves font les exercices, ni les notes de grammaire, ni le vocabulaire du jour ne sont visibles, car ils sont au verso.
Ainsi, en un seul volume, l'élève dispose d'un livre pour la classe, tout en anglais, d'un cahier d'exercices et d'un guide pour son travail personnel.

Lecture et écriture

Nous avons accordé la primauté au travail audio-oral. Mais la lecture et l'écriture ne doivent pas être négligées. Nous suggérons que, lorsqu'une leçon a été bien assimilée et pratiquée oralement, on la fasse **lire** aux élèves, silencieusement d'abord, puis à haute voix. Le livre offre de multiples possibilités de **travail écrit :** les exercices du Triliber et du « Practice », les questions qui portent sur le « Passage for comprehension ».

Les bandes magnétiques

Nous avons enregistré le texte des quatre pages de chaque chapitre, les exercices de prononciation de la deuxième page et les quatre chansons du livre, ainsi qu'une série de « drills » structuraux supplémentaires, qui peuvent être utilisés en classe ou au laboratoire de langues (le texte des « drills » se trouve dans le fichier pédagogique).

Le fichier pédagogique

Nous respectons l'indépendance et l'initiative de nos collègues. Néanmoins, il nous a paru intéressant de fournir un fichier pédagogique complet. Les professeurs y trouveront de nombreux moyens d'exploiter le livre, des notes détaillées sur la prononciation, ainsi que le texte des « drills » supplémentaires enregistrés.

Nous espérons que cette méthode, à la fois souple et systématique, facilitera votre tâche. La diversité des activités proposées devrait permettre à chaque professeur d'exploiter le livre de façon personnelle, selon le temps dont il dispose et le niveau de ses élèves.

Progression

Progression

Who are you?

CHAPTER 1

to be: singular
possessive adjectives

1

PAM: Hello!
CHARLIE: Hello! Who are you?
PAM: I'm Pam Carter.

2

CHARLIE: Who's he?
PAM: He's my brother.
His name's Dave.

3

CHARLIE: Who's she?
PAM: She's my sister.
Her name's Rosie.

4

DAVE: And who are you?
PAM & ROSIE: Yes, who are you?
CHARLIE: I'm Charlie Kipper.

Where am I?

1

CHARLIE: Where am I?
PAM: You're in our garden.

2

CHARLIE: And where's my motorbike?

3

ROSIE: It's in our house.
CHARLIE: In your house?

4

DAVE: Yes. Look!
CHARLIE: Oh dear! I'm very sorry.

Practice

Practise this dialogue :

A : Hello.
B : Hello.
A : My name's ... Who are you?
B : I'm ...

How are you?

1

PAM: Hello. 235 6471.

2

CHARLIE: Hello, Pam.
This is Charlie.

PAM: Who?

CHARLIE: Charlie Kipper.

3

PAM: Oh! Hello, Charlie.
How are you?

CHARLIE: I'm very well, thank you.
And you?

PAM: I'm very well.

4

PAM: How's your motorbike?

CHARLIE: It's fine now.

5

CHARLIE: How's your door?

PAM: It's fine now, thank you.

What time is it?

1

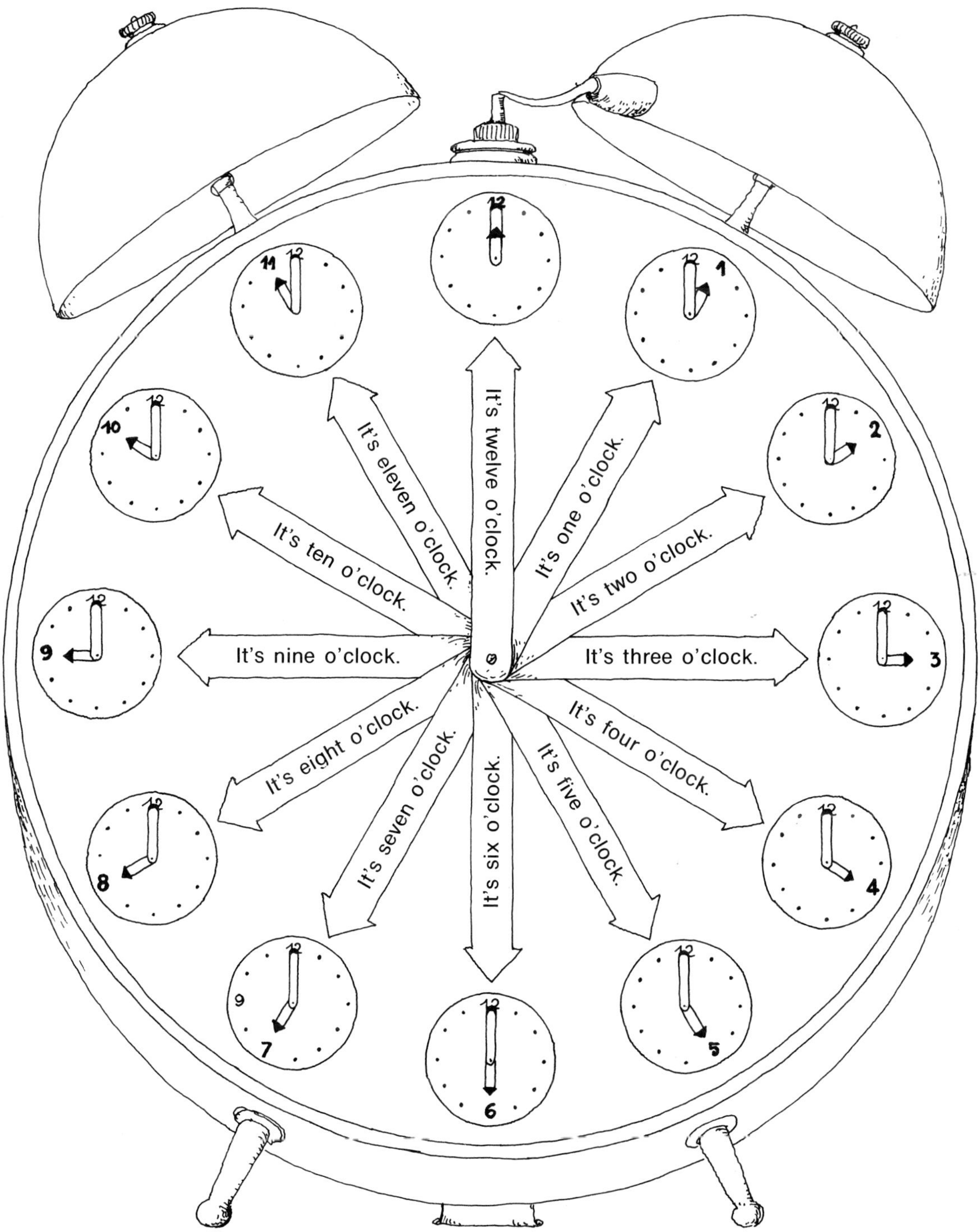

They're in Italy

CHAPTER **2**

to be: plural
short answers

1

Mr and Mrs Carter are on holiday.
They're in Italy.

2

Mr CARTER: Hello. I'm Philip Carter.
This is my wife, Marion.
We're on holiday.
We're in Italy.

3

Mrs CARTER: It's very nice here.
It's hot and sunny.

4

Mr CARTER: And it's quiet too.
Because Pam and Dave and Rosie
are at home in Brighton.

Questions

Where are Mr and Mrs Carter?
Why is it quiet?

Are Mr and Mrs Carter in Italy?
Yes, they are.

Are they in England?
No, they aren't.

Is Pam in Italy?
No, she isn't.

Is she in England?
Yes, she is.

Is Dave on holiday?
No, he isn't.

Is he at home?
Yes, he is.

Now ask and answer questions about Rosie.

Practice

Where are you?

Example: A: Are you in Italy?
B: No, I'm not. I'm in France.

ask

Are you **Is A** **Are A and B**	**at home?** **at school?** **in Italy?** **in France?** **on holiday?**

answer

Yes,	**I am.** **he is.** **she is.** **they are.**

or

No,	**I'm not. I'm...** **he isn't. He's...** **she isn't. She's...** **they aren't. They're...**

Taste this!

Pam, Dave and Rosie are at home. And here's Charlie.

1

DAVE: Hello, Charlie. Come in.

CHARLIE: Hello. How are you?

DAVE: We're fine, thank you.

2

ROSIE: Hey, Charlie. Taste this. Is it nice?

CHARLIE: Ugh! No, it isn't.

DAVE: Oh dear! It's our dinner.

3

CHARLIE: Where's your mother?

ROSIE: She isn't here. Our parents are on holiday.

4

PAM: Hello, Charlie. How's our dinner, Dave? Is it ready?

DAVE: Yes, it is. But...

PAM: Oh good. Hey, Charlie. Have dinner here.

Where's London?

2

ask

Where's	London? Paris?

answer

It's in	England. France.

ask

Is	Rome Madrid	in	Italy? Spain?

answer

Yes, it is.
No, it isn't.

or

Now ask and answer more questions.

What's this?

CHAPTER **3**

this, that,
these, those
indefinite article

1

CHARLIE: Uncle Bob, this is Pam.
PAM: Hello, Mr Kipper.
UNCLE BOB: Hello, Pam.
This is my shop. Come in.

2

PAM: What's this, Mr Kipper?
UNCLE BOB: It's a camera.
PAM: A camera?
UNCLE BOB: Yes. Look!

3

PAM: Hey, Charlie! What's that?
CHARLIE: It's an umbrella.
PAM: Really?
CHARLIE: Yes. Look!

4

PAM: What are these, Charlie?
CHARLIE: They're cups.
PAM: Cups?
CHARLIE: Yes. Look!

5

PAM: Look! What are those?
UNCLE BOB: They're bones.
PAM: Bones?
UNCLE BOB: Yes. And this is Arthur, my dog.
PAM: Hello, Arthur!

Questions

Look at picture 2:

Is it a camera?
Yes, it is.

Is it an umbrella?
No, it isn't.

Look at picture 3:

Is it an umbrella?
Yes, it is.

Is it a camera?
No, it isn't.

Look at picture 4:

Are they cups?
Yes, they are.

Are they bones?
No, they aren't.

Look at picture 5:

Are they bones?
Yes, they are.

Are they cups?
No, they aren't.

Practice

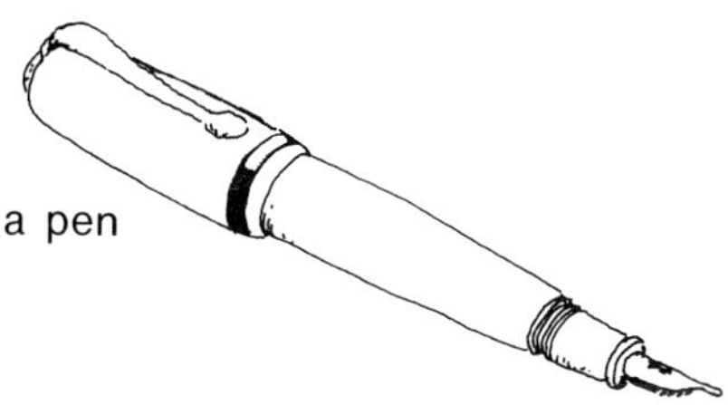

a pen

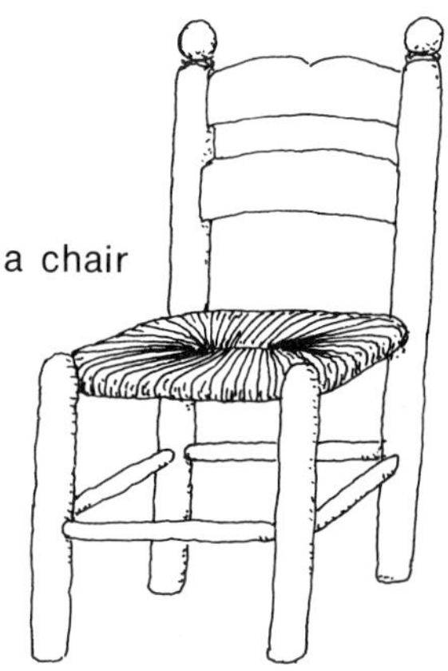

a chair

a book

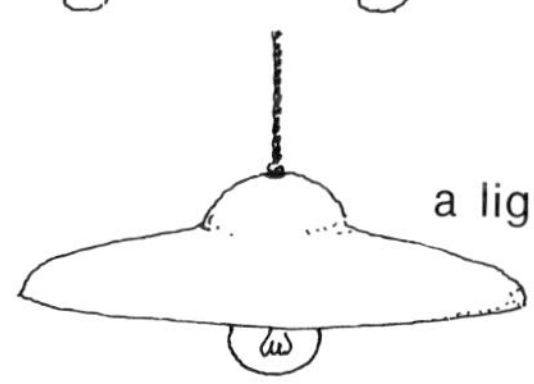

a light

a bag

a window

Look at things in your classroom and ask and answer:

What	**is** **are**	**this?** **that?** **these?** **those?**

Example: A: What's that?
B: It's a window.

Happy birthday!

Charlie and Uncle Bob are at home. It's eight o'clock.

1

CHARLIE: Good morning, Uncle Bob.
UNCLE BOB: Hello, Charlie. What's that?
CHARLIE: It's a parcel.

2

UNCLE BOB: Is it for you?
CHARLIE: No, it isn't. It's for you.
UNCLE BOB: For me? Really?
CHARLIE: Yes.

3

UNCLE BOB: What is it?
CHARLIE: It's a surprise.

4

UNCLE BOB: It's a pipe. And it's from you, Charlie. Thank you very much.
CHARLIE: Happy birthday, Uncle Bob!

What time is it?

3

Ask your friends: Excuse me. What time is it, please?

Whose hat is this?

CHAPTER **4**

whose. . . ?
"'s" possessive

1

PAM: Dave, is this your hat?
DAVE: No, it isn't. It's Charlie's hat.

2

PAM: Whose apple is that?
DAVE: It's Rosie's apple.

3

PAM: Ugh! Whose socks are these?
DAVE: They're Dad's socks.

4

PAM: Whose shoes are those?
DAVE: They're my shoes.

5

DAVE: Oh dear! Whose record is this?
PAM: It's my record!

Questions

Whose hat is it?
It's Charlie's hat.

Whose socks are they?
They're Mr Carter's socks.

Now ask and answer:

Whose/apple?
Rosie

Whose/shoes?
Dave

Whose / record?
Pam

Practice

1. *Look at things in your classroom, and ask and answer:*

Whose	**chair** **pen** **hat** **desk**	**is**	**this?** **that?**
	pens **books**	**are**	**these?** **those?**

2. *Ask and answer questions about these pictures:*

Example: A: What's this?
B: It's Uncle Bob's shop.

Look at their car!

Mr and Mrs Carter are at home again. Look at their car!

1

MRS CARTER: Look at our car!
DAVE: Go to Charlie's garage, Mum.

2

MRS CARTER: Who's Charlie?
PAM: He's our friend.
He's a mechanic.
His garage is in Park Street.

3

At Charlie's garage.

MRS CARTER: Good morning. Are you Charlie?

CHARLIE: Yes, I am. Good morning.

MRS CARTER: I'm Mrs Carter. That's my car!

4

CHARLIE: Oh dear! Go to my uncle's shop, Mrs Carter.

MRS CARTER: Is he a mechanic too?

CHARLIE: Er... no, he isn't. He's a junk collector!

What are their jobs?

4

1 What's Mr Carter's job?
He's a vet.

2 What's Mrs ... job?
She's a receptionist.

3 What's his job?
He's a policeman.

4 What's ... job?
He's a politician.

5 What's her job?
She's a secretary.

6 What's ... job?
She's a teacher.

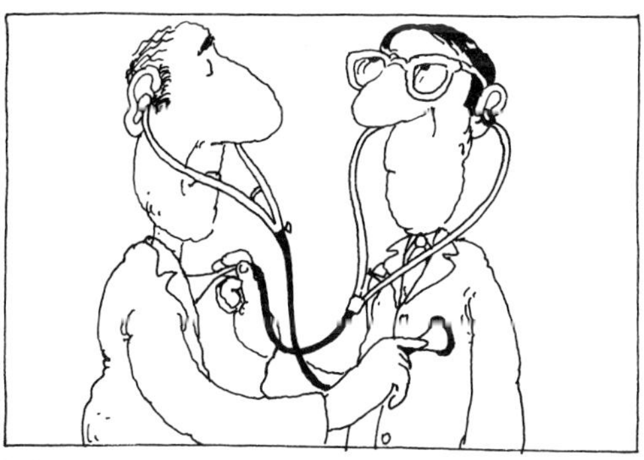

7 What are their jobs?
They're doctors.

8 What are ... jobs?
They're farmers.

Where are the keys?

CHAPTER **5**

definite article
prepositions

1

Dave's brother, Mike Carter, is in front of the supermarket. And here's his wife, Jenny.

JENNY: Hello, Mike. Where's the car?

MIKE: In the car park.

2

JENNY: Where's the car park?

MIKE: It's over there, behind the cinema.

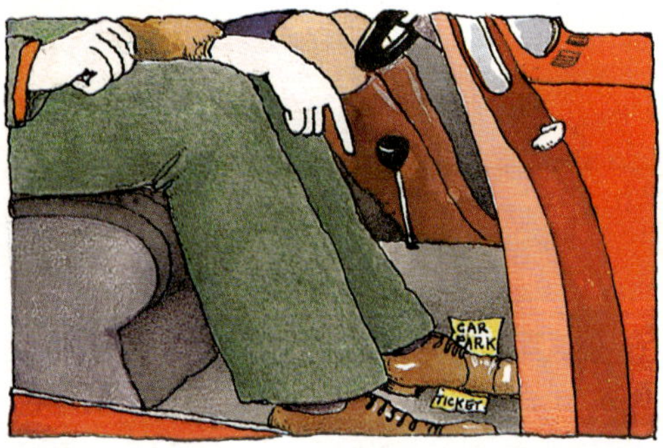

3

Mike and Jenny are in the car now.

MIKE: Where's the ticket, Jenny?

JENNY: It's on the floor, under your foot.

4

Mike and Jenny are at their flat.

MIKE: Where are the keys, Jenny?

JENNY: They aren't in my pocket, and they aren't in my bag.

5

JENNY: Oh dear! They're in the basket. They're under the shopping!

Questions

Is the car in the car park?
Yes, it is.

Is the car park behind the supermarket?
No, it isn't.

... ask and answer more questions like these.

Are the keys in Jenny's pocket?
No, they aren't.

Are they in the basket?
Yes, they are.

... ask and answer more questions like these.

Practice

1. *Look at the pictures and complete the sentences with prepositions* (in, on, under, behind, in front of):

1 Rosie's ... a policeman.

2 Arthur's ... the chair ... Uncle Bob's shop.

3 Dave's ... the cinema.

4 Pam's ... the floor.

5 Mr Carter's socks are ... the garden.

Now ask and answer questions about the pictures:

Examples: Where's Arthur?
Is Pam in the garden?

2. *Ask and answer questions about things in the classroom.*

Examples: A: Where's your pen?
B: It's on the floor.

A: Is your book on your desk?
B: No, it isn't. It's in my bag.

Be quiet!

It's twelve o'clock. Pam and Dave are in the street, near their house.

1

PAM: Where's our house?
DAVE: Sssh! Be quiet! It's very late. Here it is.
PAM: Oh yes!

2

PAM: Where's the door?
DAVE: In front of you.
PAM: Where are the keys?
DAVE: In my pocket.
PAM: Hurry up!

3
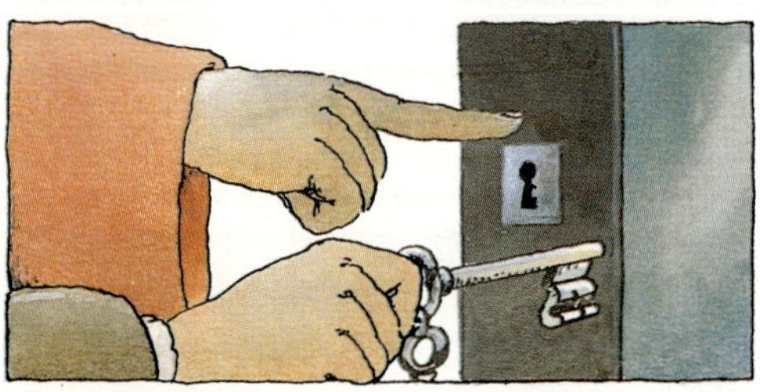

DAVE: Where's the keyhole?
PAM: Here! Look! Under my finger.

4

PAM: Now, where's the light switch?
DAVE: Here it is.
PAM: Oh! Hello, Mum.

What colour's Miss Smart?

5

1 This is Miss Smart. She's on holiday.
It's Monday. It isn't sunny.
Miss Smart's white, and her bikini's yellow.

2 It's Tuesday. Miss Smart's in a boat.
It's windy. She's green.

3 It's Wednesday. It's cold and windy.
Miss Smart's blue.

4 It's ten o'clock on Thursday, and it's sunny.
Miss Smart's pink.

5 Now it's two o'clock. It's very hot.
Miss Smart's red.

6 It's Friday. It's sunny again.
Miss Smart's brown now, but her bikini's black. The beach is very dirty!

Ask and answer questions like these:

What colour's Miss Smart on Monday?
What colour's Miss Smart's bikini on Monday?
What's the weather like in picture 2? (It's windy.)

It isn't easy, is it?

CHAPTER **6**

adjectives
question-tags

1 

Mike Carter's a sports teacher. He's at school. He's with Mr Hardy, the headmaster.

Mr HARDY: That boy's big, isn't he?

MIKE: Yes. Peter's a very big boy. And it isn't a very strong rope.

2 

Mr HARDY: Those boys are small, aren't they?

MIKE: Yes. Tim and Tony are very small. But they're strong, aren't they?

Mr HARDY: Yes, they are. Peter's very heavy.

3 

Mr HARDY: This class isn't very good, is it?

MIKE: Well, it's a difficult exercise.

4 

Mr HARDY: It isn't difficult. Watch me!

MIKE: Be careful, Mr Hardy!

5 

Mr HARDY: Oh dear!

MIKE: It isn't easy, is it, Mr Hardy?

Questions

Peter's a very big boy, isn't he?
Yes, he is.

The rope isn't very strong, is it?
No, it isn't.

Now ask and answer:

Tim and Tony are small, aren't they?

Peter's heavy, isn't he?

The class isn't very good, is it?

The exercise is difficult, isn't it?

It isn't an easy exercise, is it?

Practice

Look at the pictures and make a dialogue:

1

Example:

A: Good heavens! What a small umbrella!
B: Yes, it's very small, isn't it?

2

Example:

A: Good heavens! What big teeth!
B: Yes, they're very big, aren't they?

3

big/shoe

4

expensive / car

Now draw an object, and make a similar dialogue.

What a big dog!

Mr Carter's on the beach with Rosie. Uncle Bob's there too, with Arthur.

1

ROSIE: Dad, this is Mr Kipper.

Mr CARTER: Hello, Mr Kipper.

UNCLE BOB: Hello, Mr Carter.

ROSIE: And this is his dog, Arthur.

Mr CARTER: What a big dog!

2

UNCLE BOB: He's very friendly.

Mr CARTER: Aaagh! He's heavy too, isn't he?

UNCLE BOB: Yes, he is. Come here, Arthur! I'm sorry, Mr Carter.

3

Mr CARTER: Wait a minute! Look at his tongue. It's black.

ROSIE: And look at his teeth. They're black too.

4

UNCLE BOB: Good heavens! What is it?

Mr CARTER: It's oil.

UNCLE BOB: Yes! It's from the sea. The water's very dirty.

ROSIE: Poor Arthur. He's polluted!

Everything's cheap in Uncle Bob's shop!

6

Look at the picture and

1. *Ask and answer questions like these:*

A: How much is the clock?
B: It's two pounds.

A: How much are the records?
B: They're twenty pence.

2. *Make dialogues like this:*

A: The boots are really cheap, aren't they?
B: Yes, they're only a pound.

How much is it?

They're making a noise!

CHAPTER 7

present continuous

1

It's three o'clock on Saturday afternoon.
The Carters are at home.

Rosie's in the kitchen.
She's playing the guitar.

2

Pam's in her bedroom.
She's doing her exercises.

3

Dave's in the garage with Mike.
They're making a table.

4

Mrs Carter's in the living-room.
She's working.
She's doing the housework.

5

Mr Carter's in the living-room too.
He isn't working.
He's sitting in a chair and he's reading a book.
But it isn't easy, because everyone's making a noise!

Questions

Where's Rosie?
What's she doing?

Where are Dave and Mike?
What are they doing?

Now ask and answer questions about Pam, Mrs Carter and Mr Carter.

Is Rosie working?
No, she isn't.
Is she playing the guitar?
Yes, she is.

Are Dave and Mike working?
No, they aren't.
Are they making a table?
Yes, they are.

... ask and answer more questions like these.

Practice What a noise! Who is it?

Look at the pictures and make sentences.

1 

Example: Uncle Bob
make / a boat
It's Uncle Bob. He's making a boat.

2 

Dave and Mike
watch / television
watch / a football match

3 

Charlie
work / in his garage

4 

Arthur
sit / on the piano

5 

Mrs Carter
make / a dress

6 

Mr Carter and Rosie
do / the washing-up

What's happening?

Pam and Dave are walking along the street in Brighton. The street's full of people.

1

DAVE: Look at all those people. What are they doing?

PAM: They're looking at that woman.

DAVE: Oh yes. She's pretty, isn't she? And what an incredible car!

2

PAM: Hey! Look at that man! He's jumping out of the window into the car.

DAVE: Good heavens!

3

PAM: What's happening?

DAVE: They're making a film.

4

WOMAN: Yes, and you're standing in front of the camera.

DAVE: Oh, sorry!

What are they wearing?

7

1
It's windy.
Uncle Bob's wearing a pullover and a hat.

2
It's hot and sunny.
Rosie's wearing a dress and sunglasses.

3
It's raining.
Miss Smart's wearing a raincoat and boots.
She's carrying an umbrella.

4
It's cold.
Mr Carter's wearing a scarf and a coat.
He's carrying an electric fire.

Questions

What's Miss Smart wearing?
What's she carrying?

... ask and answer more questions like these.

Practice

a shirt

trousers

a skirt

Example: A: What are you wearing today?
B: I'm wearing a red pullover and blue trousers.

Work in pairs and make a dialogue like this.

What are they waiting for?

CHAPTER **8**

verbs + preposition
object pronouns

1

Mike and Jenny are at London airport.
They're waiting for their friends from Paris.

2

It's ten o'clock.
Mike's looking at the planes.
Jenny's looking at the sky.
It's very foggy.

3

It's eleven o'clock.
Their friends are late.
Mike's at the information desk.
An air-hostess is talking to him.

4

It's half past eleven.
The air-hostess is making an announcement.
Mike and Jenny are listening to her.
Their friends aren't coming.
It's too foggy.

5

It's twelve o'clock.
They're waiting for a taxi to the station. They're going home!

Questions

Look at picture 1:
Who are Mike and Jenny waiting for?

Picture 2:
What's Mike looking at?
What's Jenny looking at?

Picture 3:
Who's the air-hostess talking to?

Picture 4:
Who are Mike and Jenny listening to?

Picture 5:
What are they waiting for?

Practice What are they saying?

Example: Mr and Mrs Carter are standing in front of the station. They're waiting for a taxi.

Mrs Carter: Oh dear! They're waiting for a taxi too, aren't they?

Mr Carter : Yes, they are.

1

Look at these pictures and ask and answer the questions:

2

a. Where are Jenny and Pam? (bus-stop)
b. What are they waiting for? (bus)
c. What's Pam saying to Jenny?

3

a. Where are Miss Smart and her friend?
b. What's Miss Smart looking at?
c. What's Miss Smart saying to her friend?

4

a. Where are Rosie and Dave? b. What are they listening to? (radio) c. What's Charlie saying to Dave?

Listen to the wind!

It's Sunday afternoon. Pam, Charlie and Uncle Bob are in the air!

1

PAM: It's incredible, isn't it?

CHARLIE: Yes. Look at those cows, Uncle Bob.

UNCLE BOB: I'm looking at them.

CHARLIE: They're small, aren't they?

2

PAM: Good heavens! We're going very fast.

CHARLIE: Yes. It's very windy. Listen to the wind, Uncle Bob.

UNCLE BOB: I'm listening to it. It's making me ill.

3

PAM: Oh dear! Look at those trees, Charlie!

CHARLIE: Hmm. They're very near us, aren't they? Look at them, Uncle Bob.

UNCLE BOB: I'm looking at them.

4

PAM: Hey! Look at our balloon. Why are we going down?

UNCLE BOB: Because I'm pulling the rope.

CHARLIE: But why are you pulling the rope?

UNCLE BOB: Because I'm getting out!

8

Nothing's happening!

This is Sergeant Salt in police car thirty-six. Here's my report. Constable Potter's with me. We're sitting in the car. We're in the car park behind the cinema. I'm looking at the cars. Constable Potter's reading a magazine. I'm eating a sandwich. Nothing's happening. I'm waiting for my instructions.

1. Who's talking?
2. Where's Sergeant Salt?
3. Who's with him?
4. Where are they sitting?
5. Where's their car?
6. What's Sergeant Salt looking at?
7. What's Constable Potter doing?
8. What's Sergeant Salt eating?
9. What's happening?
10. What's Sergeant Salt waiting for?

The United Kingdom

Come to Brighton !

The Brighton Pavilion.

Picturepoint

Picturepoint

« The Lanes », streets in Brighton.

The pier and the beach.

Picturepoint

Revision 1

1. **Pronunciation.**
Put the words into five groups.
Example:
Group 1: ten, ready, friendly.

dog, brother, bag, shop, friendly, window, apple, England, hat, what, ten, ready, cup, colour, big.

2. *Look at the pictures in chapters 1-6, and answer these questions:*

1. On page 10, who's Pam talking to?
2. On page 14, what's Charlie wearing?
3. On page 22, what's Charlie doing?
4. On page 26, who's Mrs Carter waiting for?
5. On page 30, what are Rosie and Mr Carter doing?

3. *Complete the sentences with:*

I'm very well, thank you.
I'm very sorry.
Be quiet!
Excuse me!
Hurry up!
Be careful!

1. Sssh! ....
2. .... What's the time, please?
3. We're very late. ....
4. "Hey! You're standing on my records!" "Oh! .... ."
5. .... The water's very hot!
6. "Hello. How are you?" ".... ."

Crossword

Across

1. It's cold today. Pam's ... a scarf.
6. Five + five = ...
7. "Are you looking for your books?" "Yes, I ... ."
9. "What's that?" "It's ... umbrella."
11. "Are you English?" "Yes, we ... ."
12. Uncle Bob's on the beach and Arthur's on the beach ... .
14. What are you listening ...?
15. "My dog's ill." "... to Mr Carter, the vet."
17. I'm not coming with you, am ...?
18. Excuse me. Where's ... station, please?
20. "Where are the tickets?" "They're ... the floor."
24. "What's ... job?" "I'm a teacher."
25. "... aren't you doing this exercise?" "Because it's too difficult!"

Down

1. "... are you making?" "A dress."
2. Look ... that balloon in the sky.
3. "What colour's Charlie's hat?" "It's ... ."
4. Arthur's ... the sea.
5. Charlie's working in his ... .
8. Wait for ... . I'm not ready.
10. "Are you on holiday?" "No, I'm ... ."
13. It's ... and sunny in Italy.
16. Tim's a strong ..., isn't he?
19. Hello. ... are you?
21. "Are they listening?" "..., they aren't."
22. Is Lisbon in Spain ... in Portugal?
23. Hey! That's ... book! I'm reading it!

Waiting

It's eight o'clock in the morning.
I'm waiting at my door.
I'm listening to the radio.
What am I waiting for?

Chorus
I'm waiting for a letter.
I'm waiting here for you.
I'm waiting for an answer.
Where are you? Where are you?

It's three o'clock in the afternoon.
I'm sitting in a chair.
I'm reading all the newspapers,
But your photo isn't there.

Chorus
I'm looking at the pictures.
I'm waiting here for you.
Etc.

It's nine o'clock in the evening.
I'm standing by the telephone.
I'm listening to the silence.
Are you coming home?

Chorus
I'm listening to the silence.
I'm waiting here for you.
Etc.

It's eight o'clock in the morning.
I'm waiting at my door.
I'm looking at the people.
Who am I waiting for?

Chorus
I'm waiting and I'm listening
To the noise of a car.
I'm waiting and I'm listening.
Here you are! Here you are!

Pam can't ring the bell

CHAPTER **9**

can, can't
give + object pronoun + noun : p. 46

1 

Pam's at Uncle Bob's house.
Arthur's sitting in front of the door, so Pam can't ring the bell.

She can't move Arthur because he's too heavy.

2 

Arthur isn't sitting in front of the door now. He's playing in the garden.

So Pam can ring the bell.

3 

Uncle Bob can't hear the bell because he's singing in the bath.

4 

He isn't singing now.
He's getting dressed in his bedroom.
He can hear the bell.

5 

Uncle Bob's dressed now, and he's at the door. But he can't see Pam.

She's at the bus-stop. She's going home!

Questions

Look at picture 1:
Can Pam ring the bell?
No, she can't.
Why not?
Because Arthur's sitting in front of the door.
Can Pam move Arthur?
Why not?

Picture 2:
Can Pam ring the bell now?
Yes, she can.
Why?

Picture 3:
Can Uncle Bob hear the bell?
Why not?

Now ask and answer questions about pictures 4 and 5.

Practice

1. Why can't they do it?

1

Example: Rosie / carry / basket / heavy
Rosie can't carry the basket because it's too heavy.

2

Dave / do / exercise / difficult

3

Charlie / eat / sandwich / big

4

Miss Smart / wear / dress / small

2. *Work in pairs and practise this dialogue:*

A: Can I open the window, please?
B: Yes, of course. It's hot today, isn't it?

Now make similar dialogues, with one sentence from A and one from B.

A: 1) Can I watch television, Mum?
2) Can you carry my bag for me, please?
3) Can I play your guitar?
4) Can we have dinner now?

B: 1) Yes, O.K. But be careful!
2) No, sorry. It isn't ready.
3) No, you can't. Do the washing-up!
4) Of course. It's very heavy, isn't it?

Read this, please!

Pam's looking for a job. She's at Miss Smart's employment agency. She's sitting in the office. She's waiting for Miss Smart.

1

Miss SMART: Ah, you're here. Can you sit in the other chair, please? That's my chair.

PAM: Oh! I'm sorry, Miss Smart.

2

Miss SMART: You're looking for a job then?

PAM: Yes, I am.

Miss SMART: Good. I can give you a job. Can you cook, Miss Carter?

PAM: Yes, I can.

3

Miss SMART: Good. Can you read?

PAM: Of course I can read.

Miss SMART: Well, read this, please.

PAM: I can't read that. It's Chinese!

4

Miss SMART: Well, I'm sorry. I can't give you the job then.

PAM: What job?

Miss SMART: A Chinese restaurant's looking for a cook.

Practice What can you do?

Example: A: Can you play the piano?
B: No, I can't.

Now ask and answer:

Can you	**sing?** **cook?** **play the piano?** **draw well?** **do this exercise?** **make a dress?**

Can you make more questions like these?

At the cinema

Mrs Carter's in a queue in front of the cinema. It's half past eight in the evening. She's waiting for Mr Carter. She's looking at the other people in the queue, but she can't see him. Mr Carter's in the cinema. He's sitting in the front row and he's eating an ice-cream. He's looking for his wife but he can't see her. Now it's nine o'clock. Mr Carter's watching the film. Mrs Carter's going home.

1. Where's Mrs Carter at half past eight?
2. Who's Mrs Carter waiting for?
3. Can she see him?
4. Who's she looking at?
5. Where's Mr Carter sitting?
6. What's he eating?
7. Who's he looking for?
8. Can he see her?
9. At nine o'clock, what's Mr Carter doing?
10. What's Mrs Carter doing?

The supermarket's on fire!

CHAPTER **10**

there is, there are
let's..., don't...!

1

Pam and Dave are in the town centre.

DAVE: Look! There's a police car in front of the supermarket.

2

PAM: And there's an ambulance on the corner.

DAVE: There's a doctor over there too.

3

PAM: What's happening?

DAVE: The supermarket's on fire! Look! There are four fire-engines in the street.

4

PAM: There are two firemen on the roof.

5

DAVE: Let's stand over there, Pam.

PAM: Be careful, Dave! Don't go too near.

DAVE: But I'm taking a photograph. And I can't see with all these photographers!

Questions

Is there a police car in front of the supermarket?
Yes, there is.

Are there four fire-engines in the street?
Yes, there are.

... ask and answer more questions like these.

How many fire-engines are there in the street?
There are four.

... ask and answer more questions like this.

Practice

Newbright's a modern town.

1. *Look at the map and ask and answer questions about Newbright.*

Example: A: How many people are there in Newbright?
B: There are thirteen thousand people in Newbright.

Now draw a map of your town and ask and answer questions about it.

Example: A: How many schools are there in our town?
B: There are three schools in our town.

2. *Practise the examples, and make similar dialogues with one sentence from A and one from B.*

Example: A: Don't move!
B: Why not?
A: Because I'm taking a photograph.

A: 1) Don't give Charlie that scarf.
2) Don't wait for them.
3) Don't look.
4) Don't go too fast.
5) Don't make a noise.

B: 1) Because I'm working.
2) Because it's a surprise.
3) Because we're very late.
4) Because it's for Dave.
5) Because it's making me ill.

Example: A: Let's go to Brighton.
B: Why? Is it nice there?
A: Yes, it is.

A: 1) Let's wear our raincoats.
2) Let's stand over there.
3) Let's hurry up.
4) Let's open this parcel.
5) Let's watch television this evening.

B: 1) Why? Is it for us?
2) Why? Are we late?
3) Why? Is there a good film?
4) Why? Can't you see here?
5) Why? Is it raining?

There are fifteen rooms!

Jenny and Mike are looking for a house. There's a house for sale in Critton Street. They're looking at it with Mr Wells, the house agent.

1 

Mr WELLS: Come in. But be careful! There's a hole in the floor.

JENNY: Oh, yes!... Thank you, Mr Wells.

2 

JENNY: How many rooms are there?

Mr WELLS: There are fifteen.

MIKE: Fifteen! But that's enormous.

Mr WELLS: Yes, but it's very cheap.

3 

JENNY: What an enormous kitchen!

Mr WELLS: Yes, Mrs Carter. There are two cookers. And there's a bath too.

MIKE: A bath in the kitchen?

Mr WELLS: Well, it's a very old house, Mr Carter.

4 

JENNY: Listen! I can hear a noise. There's someone upstairs.

MIKE: Yes, there is.

Mr WELLS: No, no, no. There are always noises in old houses.

JENNY: Ah! That's why it's cheap. Let's go, Mike!

10

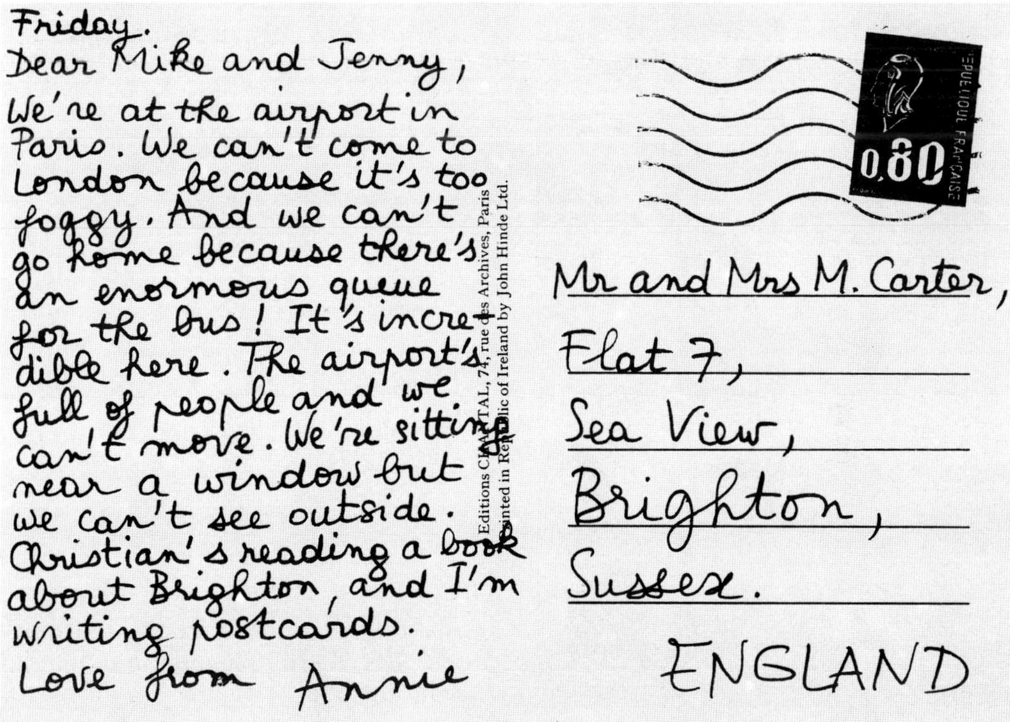

Friday.
Dear Mike and Jenny,
We're at the airport in Paris. We can't come to London because it's too foggy. And we can't go home because there's an enormous queue for the bus! It's incredible here. The airport's full of people and we can't move. We're sitting near a window but we can't see outside. Christian's reading a book about Brighton, and I'm writing postcards.
Love from Annie

Editions CHANTAL, 74, rue des Archives, Paris
Printed in Republic of Ireland by John Hinde Ltd.

0,80 REPUBLIQUE FRANÇAISE

Mr and Mrs M. Carter,
Flat 7,
Sea View,
Brighton,
Sussex.
ENGLAND

1. Where are Annie and Christian?
2. What's the weather like?
3. Can they come to London? Why not?
4. Why can't they go home?
5. Why can't Annie and Christian move?
6. Where are they sitting?
7. Can they see outside? Why not?
8. What's Christian doing?
9. What's Annie doing?

Practice

What's Mike and Jenny's address?

Now imagine you're giving an English friend your address.
Spell the name of your street and the name of your town in English.

Can you spell your name in English?

Let's make a chicken pie

CHAPTER 11

some, any, a lot of

1

Charlie and Uncle Bob are in the kitchen. They're cooking their lunch.

UNCLE BOB: What's in the fridge?

CHARLIE: There's some chicken.

UNCLE BOB: Good. Let's make a chicken pie.

2

UNCLE BOB: Is there any butter, Charlie?

CHARLIE: Yes, there is.

3

UNCLE BOB: Are there any tomatoes?

CHARLIE: No, there aren't any tomatoes. But there are some onions and some carrots.

UNCLE BOB: Well, give me the onions and carrots then.

4

UNCLE BOB: Can you give me the salt please, Charlie?

CHARLIE: Oh dear! There isn't any salt. But there's some pepper.

UNCLE BOB: Well, give me the pepper then, please.

5

UNCLE BOB: Taste it. Is it good?

CHARLIE: Aaagh! It isn't bad. But there's a lot of pepper!

Questions

Is there any chicken?
Yes, there is.

Are there any tomatoes?
No, there aren't.

... ask and answer more questions like these.

What's in the pie?
There's some chicken in the pie.

Now complete the list.

Practice

1. Why are they surprised?

Example: cook / people / restaurant
The cook's surprised because there aren't any people in the restaurant.

1

2
Miss Smart / pictures / magazine

3
Sergeant Salt / chicken / sandwich

4
Mike / water / swimming-pool

5
Arthur / bones / hole

2. *Make five true sentences with these words.*

There's **There are**	**a** **some** **a lot of**	**book(s)** **picture(s)** **money** **plane(s)** **chair(s)** **car(s)** **bus(es)** **water**	**in the sky.** **in the sea.** **in my bag.** **in my desk.** **in this town.** **in the street.** **at home.** **in the classroom.**

A lot of old junk

Mrs Carter's in the garden near the garage. She's making a fire. Charlie's there too.

1

CHARLIE: That's a big fire, Mrs Carter.

Mrs CARTER: Yes. There's a lot of old junk in the garage. I'm burning it.

2

CHARLIE: Hey! Don't burn those books, Mrs Carter.

Mrs CARTER: Why not?

CHARLIE: Uncle Bob's looking for some books for his shop.

Mrs CARTER: Really? Well, you can take them. Here you are.

3

CHARLIE: Are there any old clothes?

Mrs CARTER: Yes. Look! I can give you a lot of old clothes. Here you are.

4

CHARLIE: Can I take this coat?

Mrs CARTER: Oh dear!

CHARLIE: What's the matter, Mrs Carter?

Mrs CARTER: That's my husband's new coat!

11

Where are all the men?

It's seven o'clock on Wednesday evening. Miss Smart's walking home from her office. She's very surprised, because there aren't any people in the street. There are some buses, but there aren't any men in them. There are only women. She can see a policeman in front of her. But wait a minute! It isn't a policeman. It's a police-woman. Where are all the men in Brighton? They're at home. There's a football match on television.

1. What time is it?
2. What day is it?
3. Is Miss Smart in her office?
4. What's she doing?
5. Why is she surprised?
6. Are there any men in the buses?
7. Is there a policeman in the street?
8. Where are all the men this evening?
9. What's on television?

He's got a knife!

CHAPTER **12**

have got

1

Sergeant Salt's at the police station. He's questioning a man about the fire at the supermarket. The man's emptying his pockets.

SERGEANT: What have you got in your pockets?

MAN: I've got a knife.

SERGEANT: He's got a knife, Constable Potter.

2

MAN: I've got a fork.

SERGEANT: He's got a fork, Constable Potter.

MAN: I've got some salt.

SERGEANT: He's got some salt.

MAN: I've got a box of matches.

SERGEANT: Ah! Interesting! He's got some matches, Constable Potter. But he hasn't got any cigarettes.

4

MAN: And I've got some fish under my hat.

SERGEANT: He's got some fish under his hat.

5

MAN: And you've got a table. That's good. And you've got a cooker too. So now I can have my lunch!

Questions

What has the man got in his pockets?
What has he got under his hat?
What have the policemen got at the police station?

Has the man got a knife?
Yes, he has.

Has he got any cigarettes?
No, he hasn't.

Have the policemen got a cooker?
Yes, they have.

... ask and answer more questions like these.

Practice

1. *Make true sentences about the people in this book.*

Example: Charlie's got a motorbike.

2. *Example:* Dave's got a postcard, but Rosie hasn't.

Now make true sentences about yourself and your friends.

Example: Paul's got a lot of records, but I haven't.

3. *Ask and answer these questions:*

What have you got	**in** **on**	**your**	**pocket?** **bag?** **desk?**

Example: A: What have you got on your desk?
B: I've got some books and an apple.

Customers can be difficult!

Pam's got a new job in a chemist's shop.

1

PAM: Good morning, sir. Can I help you?

CUSTOMER: Yes. Can I have a toothbrush, please?

PAM: Certainly, sir.

2

PAM: Oh, they're on the top shelf. Just a minute, sir.

CUSTOMER: Be careful!

3

PAM: Here you are. What colour, sir? Red, green, blue, yellow, brown, black or white?

CUSTOMER: Er... you haven't got a pink toothbrush, have you?

PAM: Pink? Oh. Er... just a minute, sir.

4

PAM: Here you are, sir. That's forty pence, please.

CUSTOMER: Oh dear!

PAM: What's the matter, sir?

CUSTOMER: I haven't got any money. My wallet's at home.

What are they like?

12

What's Charlie like?

He's tall.
He's got short, black hair.

What's Pam like?

She's quite tall.
She's got long, blond hair.

What's Mr Carter like?

He's short and quite fat.
He's got a moustache.

What's Miss Smart like?

She's thin.
She's got glasses.

Practice

1. POLICE NOTICE

The police are looking for this man. What's he like?

2. *Ask and answer these questions:*

What's your	**friend** **mother** **brother** **sister**	**like?**

Example: A: What's your friend John like?
B: My friend John's tall and thin. He's got brown hair. He's got glasses.

What do they do every day?

CHAPTER 13

simple present

1

Listen to Mrs Carter :

MRS CARTER: Every day I get up at seven o'clock.

My husband gets up at half past seven.

2

We have breakfast at eight o'clock.

I have coffee for breakfast.

Philip doesn't like coffee, so he has tea.

3

I'm a hotel receptionist. I work from two to six.

Philip's a vet. He works in his surgery from nine to half past five.

4

Philip doesn't work on Sunday.
He stays in bed in the morning.

I don't stay in bed. I wash the car.

Questions

What time does Mr Carter get up?
What time do Mr and Mrs Carter have breakfast?
What does Mr Carter have for breakfast?
Where does Mr Carter work?
When does he work?
What does he do on Sunday?

Now ask and answer questions about Mrs Carter.

Does Mrs Carter get up at seven?
Yes, she does.

Does Mr Carter get up at seven?
No, he doesn't. He gets up at half past seven.

... ask and answer more questions like these.

Practice

1. ask

Do you **Does your friend**	**like**	**dogs?** **tea?** **chicken?** **English records?** **ice-cream?**

answer

Yes,	**I do.** **he/she does.**

or

No,	**I don't.** **he/she doesn't.**

Can you find more questions and answers like these?

2. *Ask and answer these questions. Make true sentences about yourself.*

What time **When**	**do you**	**get up?** **have breakfast?** **have lunch?** **have dinner?** **go to school?** **go home?** **go to bed?**

Are you	**getting up** **having breakfast** **having lunch** **having dinner** **going to school** **going home** **going to bed**	**now?**

Examples: A: What time do you have lunch?
B: I have lunch at twelve o'clock.
A: Are you having lunch now?
B: No, I'm not. I'm having an English lesson now.

What a coincidence!

It's raining. Mike's driving to work. A man's standing at the bus-stop, but there aren't any buses.

1

MIKE: Hello. Can I give you a lift?

MAN: Oh, yes please. I want to go to Richmond Road.

MIKE: Fine. Get in.

2

MIKE: You aren't English, are you?

MAN: No, I'm not. I'm French. I come from Brittany. Do you speak French?

MIKE: No, I don't!

3

MIKE: Do you like Brighton?

MAN: Yes, I do. I like it very much. There are a lot of things to do here.

4

MIKE: Are you on holiday?

MAN: No, I'm not. I've got a job at Grove School.

MIKE: Really? I work there. I'm the sports teacher.

MAN: What a coincidence! I'm the new French teacher!

13

They have lunch at midnight!

On Saturday Sergeant Salt goes to work at eight o'clock in the evening! He's got a car, but he walks to the police station. He says "Good evening" to Constable Potter, and they have a cup of coffee. They get into police car thirty-six and they drive round Brighton. They work all night. They have lunch at midnight! They finish work at six o'clock on Sunday morning. Sergeant Salt walks home. The streets are very quiet because everyone's in bed. He arrives home at half past six. But he doesn't go to bed. He makes breakfast for his wife.

1. What time does Sergeant Salt go to work on Saturday?
2. Does he go to work by car?
3. What does he say to Constable Potter?
4. Do they have a cup of tea?
5. Do they stay at the police station?
6. When do they work?
7. What time do they have their lunch?
8. When do they finish work?
9. Does Sergeant Salt drive home?
10. Why are the streets quiet?
11. What time does he arrive home?
12. Does he go to bed?

It's often difficult for Arthur

CHAPTER **14**

frequency adverbs
omission of conjunction "that": p. 66

1

It isn't easy to live with Uncle Bob and Charlie.

Uncle Bob always sings in the bath.

2

Charlie never closes the front door.

3

Uncle Bob often drops ash on the floor.

4

Charlie sometimes comes home late with his friends.
They always make a noise.

5

Arthur usually sleeps in the kitchen. But tonight he's sleeping in the garden, because it's quiet there!

Questions

Does Uncle Bob sing in the bath?
Yes, he always sings in the bath.

Does Charlie close the front door?
No, he never closes the front door.

... ask and answer more questions like these.

Does Uncle Bob always sing in the bath?
Yes, he does.

Does Charlie ever close the front door?
No, he doesn't.

... ask and answer more questions like these.

Practice

1. What food do you like?

Work in pairs and practise this dialogue:

A: Do you like tea?
B: No, I don't. I never drink tea.

A: Do you like apples?
B: Yes, I do. I often have an apple for lunch.

Now work in pairs and make a similar dialogue with: chicken, coffee, ice-cream, spaghetti, tomatoes, fish.

2. ask

What	**do** **does**	**you** **your friends** **your parents** **your brother** **your sister**	**do**	**in the evening?** **at the weekend?** **on Saturday?**

answer

I **He** **She** **They**	**usually** **always** **often** **sometimes**	...

Example: A: What do you do at the weekend?
B: I usually stay at home.

The Brighton Regatta

There's a regatta in Brighton today. Uncle Bob and Charlie are in their boat, Sunlight. Pam and Dave are watching the race.

1 

PAM: What's Mr Kipper's boat like, Dave?

DAVE: I think it's got red sails. Look at the programme, Pam.

PAM: The programme says it's number forty-six.

2 

DAVE: I can see it. There it is! Look, Pam, near the finishing flag.

PAM: Oh yes. And there's only one boat in front of it. Come on, Sunlight!

3 

In Sunlight

CHARLIE: There's only one boat in front of us, Uncle Bob.

UNCLE BOB: I know. It's Mr Hardy, the headmaster of Grove School. He wins this race every year.

CHARLIE: Well, not this year. Come on, Sunlight!

4 

CHARLIE: Uncle Bob! Look!
Mr Hardy's in the water.

UNCLE BOB: Good heavens! Charlie, I think we're winning.

CHARLIE: We are winning, Uncle Bob! We're first.

UNCLE BOB: Incredible! Sunlight's usually last!

14

Practice What do you think?

Ask and answer these questions:

1. Do you think English is easy or difficult?
2. Do you think your school's too big or too small?
3. Do you think clothes are cheap or expensive?
4. Do you think this exercise is too long or too short?

Now answer these questions with "I think...":

Example: A: What number's the Carters' house?
B: I think it's number eighteen.

1. What number's Sergeant Salt's police car?
2. What number's Mike and Jenny's flat?
3. What colour's Charlie's hat?
4. What does Mr Carter drink at breakfast?

The Sussex Car Rally

Everyone thinks Miss Smart's a very quiet person. She doesn't often go out in the evening. She usually stays at home at the weekend too. But today's different. It's Saturday, and Miss Smart's in her car. She's got a big map in her pocket. She's watching a man with a flag, and she's waiting. The man's standing in front of a long row of cars. Miss Smart's number seven. Now all the cars are moving. What a noise! What's happening? Well, it's the Sussex Car Rally. And Miss Smart usually wins.

1. What does everyone think of Miss Smart?
2. Does she often go out in the evening?
3. What does she usually do at the weekend?
4. What day is it?
5. Where's Miss Smart?
6. What has she got in her pocket?
7. What's Miss Smart doing?
8. Where's the man standing?
9. There's a number on Miss Smart's car. What is it?
10. Why is there a noise?
11. What's happening?
12. Is Miss Smart usually first or last?

Martin

1

London

2

Martin

1. The Houses of Parliament and Big Ben.

2. English umbrellas — they come out when the sun goes in.

3. Portobello Road — here you can buy everything, from a flag to a fireman's hat!

4. These people are listening to someone at Speakers' Corner in Hyde Park.

5. « Hurry up! You're late! » Big Ben's watching a big, red London bus.

3 

Martin
Martin

4 

Martin

5 

Revision 2

Find the differences.

Picture 1 and picture 2 are different. Why? Find six things.

Crossword

Across

1. "... you sing?" "Yes, very well."
4. I carry my books to school in a ... .
8. "Is that a ... coat?" "Oh no! It's very old."
10. Be quiet! I'm listening ... the radio.
12. "What's Mr Carter's job?" "He's a ... ."
14. What's ... matter?
15. Maria's from Italy. ... lives in Rome.
17. The customer's coming out ... the chemist's shop.
18. There ... a lot of people on the beach today.
20. "Does Uncle Bob work in an office?" "No, ... doesn't."
21. I can't make a fire. There aren't ... matches.
23. The postcard's for ... . That's my name and address.
24. Arthur drinks tea and he ... potatoes!
26. Mike goes to work ... car.

Down

1. Can I have ... apple, please?
3. I ... eat onions. They make me ill.
5. What are you looking ...?
6. It's raining. Has Pam ... her umbrella?
7. ... are two big holes in my sock!
9. "Are you ready?" "Yes, ... are."
11. ... there any money in your pocket?
13. Are you talking ... me?
16. You haven't got two pounds, ... you?
19. English isn't difficult. It's ...!
20. Miss Smart's wearing a pink ... and a blue coat.
22. "Do you want a cup of coffee?" "..., please."
23. Can you see ... scarf? I can't find it.
25. Rosie's making a noise, ... Dave can't hear the television.

Christopher King

Christopher King's a new pop star,
But he can't sing or play the guitar.
He's got money; he's got everything.
There's a future for Christopher King.
Oh yeah! Oh yeah! Oh yeah!
All the windows are black in his big, black car,
But Christopher King can't play the guitar.

Everyone listens to Christopher King.
They don't want to know that he can't sing.
They hear his records on the radio;
They all want tickets for Chris's T.V. show.
Whoah, whoah! Whoah, whoah! Whoah, whoah!
Are you sure that money gives you everything?
I don't know. Ask Christopher King.

When he walks along the street, his fans are there.
They pull his clothes; they pull his hair.
They know his number on the telephone.
They ring his doorbell when they think he's at home.
Whoah, whoah! Whoah, whoah! Whoah, whoah!
Close all the doors and the windows too.
A pop star just can't live like you.

Christopher King isn't happy, I know.
With all his fans, where can he go?
What's the matter with Christopher King?
Can't his money buy him everything?
No, no! No, no! No, no!
He wants to be a farmer, but his fans say "No!"
What can he do? Where can he go?

It isn't ours!

CHAPTER **15**

possessive pronouns
give/show it to him

1

Sergeant Salt's at the police station. The Inspector's talking to him.

INSPECTOR: Sergeant Salt! There's a cheese and tomato sandwich on my desk. Is it yours?

SERGEANT: No, Inspector. It isn't mine.

2

INSPECTOR: Well, show it to Constable Potter. Perhaps it's his.

SERGEANT: It can't be Constable Potter's. He doesn't like tomatoes.

3

INSPECTOR: Well, give it to Constable Peabody. Perhaps it's hers.

SERGEANT: It can't be Constable Peabody's. She never eats cheese. It makes her ill.

4

INSPECTOR: Well, whose is it then?

SERGEANT: I don't know, Inspector. Let's write it in the lost property book.

INSPECTOR: Don't be silly, Sergeant. I know! Let's eat it. I'm hungry.

5

SERGEANT: But it isn't ours!

INSPECTOR: I know. But if a sandwich is in someone's stomach, it doesn't exist. And if it doesn't exist, it isn't anyone's, is it?

Questions

Whose sandwich is it? Is it the Inspector's?
No, it isn't his.

Now ask and answer questions about Sergeant Salt, Constable Potter and Constable Peabody.

Practice

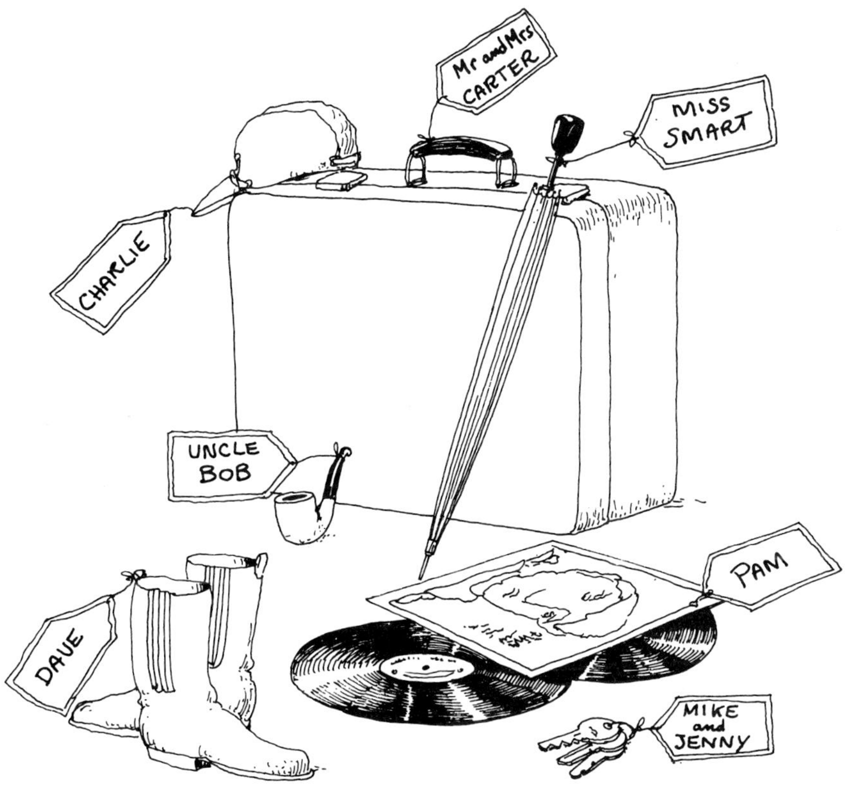

1. *Look at the picture and make dialogues like this:*

Example: A: Whose case is it?
B: It's Mr and Mrs Carter's. Can you give it to them, please?

2. *Now ask and answer questions about things in the classroom.*

Example: A; Is this your book?
B: No, it isn't mine. Mine's on my desk. Show it to C. Perhaps it's hers.
A: Is this book yours?
C: Yes, it is. Thank you very much.

Work in pairs and make a similar dialogue. Change the underlined words.

That case is mine!

Uncle Bob's going to London. He's at the station. He's buying his ticket.

1

UNCLE BOB: A return ticket to London, please.

BOOKING CLERK: Certainly, sir. That's four pounds twenty, please.

UNCLE BOB: Four pounds twenty. Here you are.

2

MAN: Excuse me. I think you've got my case.

UNCLE BOB: Oh really? I'm very sorry. Ah, mine's over there.

3

WOMAN 1: Hey! That case is ours. Give it to me.

WOMAN 2: Call the police, Alice!

UNCLE BOB: Wait a minute! I'm sure this case is mine. Look! That porter's got yours.

4

WOMAN 2: Oh yes. Come on, Alice. Run! Hey, stop! You've got our case.

UNCLE BOB: Oh dear! A nightdress! This isn't my case. It's theirs. And the porter's got mine!

15

Call the vet!

Mr Carter's job isn't always easy. It's often very difficult to know why an animal's ill. A dog can't say to the vet: "I've got a bad tooth", or "I can't see very well, doctor." But Mr Carter's a very good vet, and he usually finds the answer. That's why he's got a lot of customers. The farmers near Brighton always telephone Mr Carter when their animals are ill. Sometimes his telephone rings when he's in bed, because a cow isn't well. He gets up, gets dressed and goes out at midnight. At home, his surgery's always full. His customers think he's incredible. One woman often comes to the surgery and says her cat's fine, but she isn't very well. So today Mr Carter's making a notice for his door. It says: "I can listen to your cat's problems; but I'm sorry, I can't listen to yours."

1. Why isn't Mr Carter's job easy?
2. Can a dog answer the question: "What's the matter?"?
3. Why has Mr Carter got a lot of customers?
4. When do the farmers telephone Mr Carter?
5. Does his telephone ever ring late in the evening?
6. Does Mr Carter ever work at night?
7. Are there usually a lot of people in his surgery?
8. What do his customers think of him?
9. Does the woman come to the surgery because her cat's ill?
10. What's Mr Carter doing today?
11. What does the notice say?

You mustn't miss it!

CHAPTER **16**

present continuous: future meaning
must, mustn't

Charlie wants to see a film called « Big Fish ». It's Monday, and he's talking to Pam on the telephone.

1

CHARLIE: What are you doing tomorrow evening, Pam? Can you come to the cinema?

PAM: No, I'm sorry Charlie. I can't. I'm washing my hair tomorrow evening.

2

CHARLIE: But you must come, Pam. They say it's a great film. Wash your hair on Wednesday.

PAM: I'm sorry, Charlie. I can't. I'm going out to dinner on Wednesday.

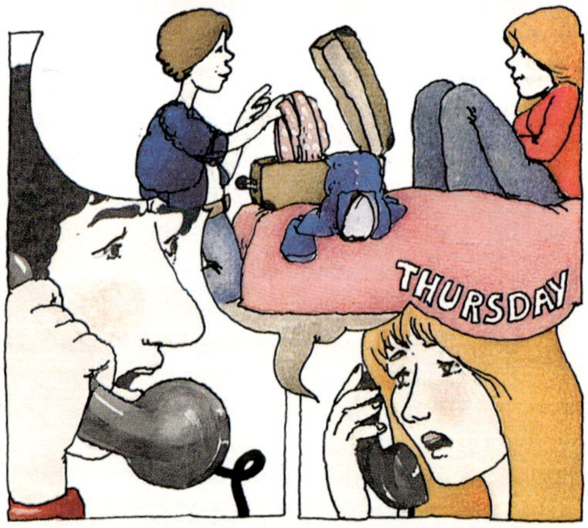

3

CHARLIE: Oh! Well, are you free on Thursday then?

PAM: No, I'm not. I'm seeing a friend on Thursday.

CHARLIE: See her another evening.

PAM: I'm sorry, Charlie. I can't. She's going on holiday on Friday.

4

CHARLIE: Listen, Pam. The film's only here for a week. You mustn't miss it.

PAM: Well, I can come on Friday, Charlie. I'm not doing anything on Friday.

CHARLIE: Oh... er, well I'm not free on Friday. I'm going to a football match.

Questions

What's Charlie doing on Tuesday evening?
He isn't doing anything.

What's Pam doing on Tuesday evening?
She's washing her hair.

Now ask and answer questions about Wednesday, Thursday and Friday.

Why must Pam see "Big Fish"?
Because they say it's a great film.

Why must she see the film this week?

Practice

1. Mrs Carter's very busy next week. She's at work every afternoon at the White Tree Hotel, and she's doing something every morning. Look at her diary.

Ask and answer questions about Mrs Carter's week.

Example: A: What's Mrs Carter doing on Monday morning?
B: She's going to the doctor's at ten thirty.

26 Monday
10.30 Go to doctor's

27 Tuesday
Buy a new coat for Philip

28 Wednesday
11.00 Have coffee at Jenny's

29 Thursday
Take the car to the garage

30 Friday
Go shopping

2. *Look at these notices and make sentences with "must" or "mustn't".*

a) Outside the headmaster's office	SILENCE
b) In Mr Carter's surgery	Please close the door
c) In the car park	Don't forget to take a ticket
d) At the White Tree Hotel	Reception. Please ring the bell
e) In Miss Smart's employment agency	Don't open the window
f) In the town centre	Be careful! Don't drive too fast

Example: *a)* You mustn't talk when you're outside the headmaster's office.
You must be quiet.

I'm getting up early

It's eleven o'clock at night. Dave's watching television in the living-room. Mrs Carter's at the door.

1

Mrs CARTER: Dave! You must go to bed. It's very late.

DAVE: It's only eleven o'clock, Mum. And I must see the end of this film.

2

Mrs CARTER: But don't forget, you're taking an exam tomorrow.

DAVE: Yes, I know, Mum.

3

DAVE: And I'm getting up early too.

Mrs CARTER: What time are you getting up?

DAVE: Three o'clock.

Mrs CARTER: Three o'clock!

4

Mrs CARTER: You must be mad! You can't revise for your exam at three in the morning.

DAVE: I know I can't. There's a boxing match from America on T.V. Joe Bix is fighting Sam Sly. I mustn't miss that!

16

Talk, talk, talk!

Mr Newton's a politician. He's a Member of Parliament. He lives in Brighton, and everyone knows him. He's tall and thin and he's got red hair. He always wears green trousers and he drives a small, yellow car. Mr Newton's very busy next weekend. He's got a lot to do. On Saturday morning he's opening a new supermarket. In the afternoon he's visiting a factory. And in the evening he and his wife are having dinner with two hundred firemen. Mr Newton's busy on Sunday too. He's talking about his job on the radio in the morning. In the afternoon he's having tea with some old people in Brighton. On Sunday evening he's staying at home. He's writing another chapter of his autobiography. It's called "Talk, talk, talk!"

1. What's Mr Newton's job?
2. Where does he live?
3. What's Mr Newton like?
4. What colour's his car?
5. Is he free next weekend?
6. What's he doing on Saturday morning?
7. Is he busy on Saturday afternoon?
8. What are he and his wife doing in the evening?
9. When's he talking about his job on the radio?
10. Who's he seeing on Sunday afternoon?
11. Is he going out on Sunday evening?
12. What's his autobiography called?

It's better than yours

CHAPTER **17**

comparatives

1

Rosie's visiting her brother, Mike. They're in the street outside Mike's flat. Mike's neighbour, Jack, has got a new car. Rosie's looking at it.

ROSIE: Hey, Mike! Look at Jack's new car.

MIKE: I know. Very big and very expensive.

ROSIE: It's bigger than yours, isn't it?

MIKE: It's more expensive than ours too.

2

ROSIE: Hey, Mike! Look at the boot.

MIKE: I know. It's enormous, isn't it?

ROSIE: It's nearly as long as your car.

MIKE: Yes, but our car's easier to park.

3

ROSIE: Hey, Mike! Look at the seats. They're more comfortable than yours.

MIKE: O.K. Our seats aren't as comfortable as Jack's. But I like our car. It's a good car.

ROSIE: It isn't as good as Jack's. His is a lot better than yours, Mike.

4

MIKE: Rosie, do you want to walk home?

Questions

Is Mike's car as big as Jack's?
No, it isn't as big as Jack's.
No, Jack's car's bigger than Mike's.

Now answer these questions in the same way:
Is Mike's car as expensive as Jack's?
Is the boot as long as Jack's?
Is Jack's car as easy to park as Mike's?
Are Mike's seats as comfortable as Jack's?
Is Mike's car as good as Jack's?

Practice

1. *Compare these two planes.*

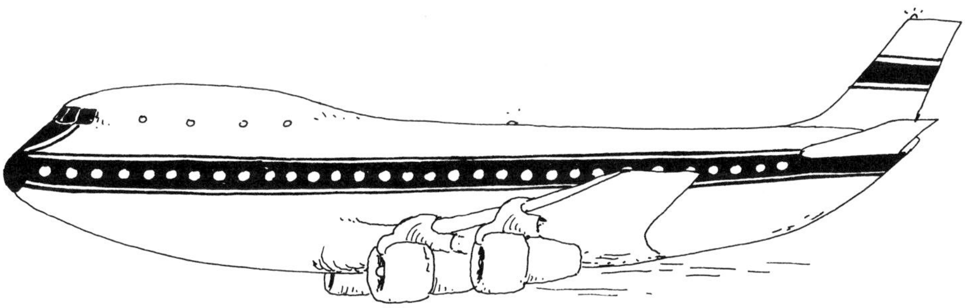

Examples: The first plane's more modern than the second.
The second plane isn't as modern as the first.

Use these adjectives: quiet, fast, old, interesting, cold, big, expensive, small, heavy, long, comfortable.

2. *Ask and answer these questions:*

How old are you? (I'm fourteen.)
How tall are you? (I'm one metre sixty.)

Are you as	**old** **heavy** **intelligent** **strong** **tall**	**as your**	**teacher?** **father?** **friend?** **sister?** **brother?**

Examples: A: Are you as tall as your brother?
B: Yes. In fact, I'm taller than him.

A: Are you as heavy as your sister?
B: No. She's heavier than me.

Miss Smart's hat

It's very windy today. Miss Smart's hat's in a tree. She's near Uncle Bob's shop. Perhaps Uncle Bob can help her.

1

MISS SMART: Excuse me, Mr Kipper. My hat's in a tree. Have you got a ladder?

UNCLE BOB: Yes, I have. Just a minute.

2

UNCLE BOB: Here you are.

MISS SMART: Oh... er, it's very heavy, isn't it? Can you carry it for me? You're stronger than me.

UNCLE BOB: Yes, all right. But I must be quick. I've got a lot of customers.

3

UNCLE BOB: There! The ladder's ready. Be careful, Miss Smart.

MISS SMART: Oh dear. It's very high, isn't it? Mr Kipper, can you... er...

UNCLE BOB: All right. But someone must serve my customers.

MISS SMART: Don't worry! I can do that.

4

UNCLE BOB: I've got your hat for you, Miss Smart.

MISS SMART: Oh, you're wonderful, Mr Kipper. Thank you. Oh, and I've got twenty pounds for you.

UNCLE BOB: Twenty pounds! You're more persuasive than me, Miss Smart.

MISS SMART: You know, Mr Kipper, I think we work well together!

17

The Boxing Match

Good evening, ladies and gentlemen. I'm speaking to you from Madison Square Garden in New York. All the seats here are full, because tonight Joe Bix is fighting Sam Sly. Everyone's waiting for these two great boxers. And here they are! They're coming into the ring now. Sam Sly isn't as heavy as Joe Bix. And Joe's stronger and taller than Sam. But Sam Sly's very fast. He's a lot faster than Joe Bix. Are they ready? Yes, they are. There's the bell! And they're starting. Good heavens! Joe Bix is on the floor. The referee's counting, but Joe Bix isn't moving. He can't get up! Now the referee's making an announcement. It's the end of the fight. Sam Sly's the winner.

1. What's happening tonight?
2. Are there a lot of people at Madison Square Garden?
3. Who's everyone waiting for?
4. Is Sam Sly as heavy as Joe Bix?
5. Is Sam as strong as Joe? Is he as tall?
6. Is Joe as fast as Sam?
7. There's the bell! What are the two boxers doing?
8. Where's Joe Bix?
9. What's the referee doing?
10. Is Joe Bix getting up?
11. What's the referee doing now?
12. Who's the winner?

What are you going to do?

CHAPTER **18**

future: going to

1

It's the weekend and the Carters are at home. Mrs Carter's very busy.

ROSIE: What are you going to do with those newspapers, Mum?

Mrs CARTER: I'm going to cover the furniture.

2

DAVE: What are you going to do with that ladder, Mum?

Mrs CARTER: I'm going to paint the living-room.

3

PAM: What are you going to do with that hammer, Mum?

Mrs CARTER: I'm going to put some pictures on the wall.

4

Mr CARTER: Marion! What are you going to do with that knife?

Mrs CARTER: Don't worry, dear. I'm going to cut the meat.

Questions

What's Mrs Carter going to do with the newspapers?
She's going to cover the furniture.

... ask and answer more questions like this.

Is Mrs Carter going to cover the furniture?
Yes, she is.

... ask and answer more questions like this.

Practice

1. What are they going to do?

1

2

3

4

2. *Can you complete this conversation? What does A say?*

A:
B: Yes, I know. What are you going to buy him?
A:
B: Socks! That isn't very interesting.
A:
B: I'm going to give him a guitar.
A:
B: Oh, I'm not going to buy it. I'm going to give him mine. I never play it.

Aren't you going to stop him?

Rosie and Dave are in the chemist's shop where Pam works. Pam's busy at the moment, so they're waiting for her.

1

ROSIE: Hey, Dave! Look at that man over there.

DAVE: Why? What's the matter?

ROSIE: He's got five pairs of sunglasses in his hand. He's going to put them in his pocket!

DAVE: Don't be silly, Rosie. He's going to try them on.

ROSIE: No, he isn't.

2

DAVE: Well, tell Pam.

ROSIE: No, she's too busy. Look! He's walking towards the door. Hurry up, Dave!

DAVE: What do you mean?

ROSIE: Aren't you going to stop him?

DAVE: No, I'm not.

ROSIE: Well, I am.

3

ROSIE: Hey, you! What are you doing with those sunglasses?

MAN: Pardon? Are you talking to me, young lady?

PAM: Rosie! I'm sorry, Mr Barker. This is my sister. Rosie, this is Mr Barker, the manager.

ROSIE: The manager!

MAN: Yes, the manager. Now you must excuse me. I'm going to put these sunglasses in the window.

18

Here are my decisions

It's the end of December. The manager of a big clothes factory is talking to his employees.
"Ladies and gentlemen, we all know things are difficult at the moment. We aren't making a lot of money. In fact, we aren't making any money. What can we do? I know you all want to help, so I'm going to give you lower salaries. And you're all going to sell your cars, and come to work by bicycle. I'm going to help too, of course. I'm going to sell one of my cars. Next year isn't going to be easy. We must make more clothes. So we're all going to work six days a week, and I'm going to work six weeks a year. Well, those are my decisions. Oh, where are you all going?"

1. What month is it?
2. Who's the manager talking to?
3. Are things easy at the moment?
4. Are they making a lot of money?
5. Is the manager going to give his employees higher salaries?
6. Are they going to come to work by car?
7. Is the manager going to sell all his cars?
8. What must they do next year?
9. How many days a week are they going to work?
10. Is the manager going to work every week next year?

If you stand up, you'll fall!

CHAPTER **19**

future : will, won't

1

Dave and Charlie are in the country. They're on Charlie's motorbike.

DAVE: I'm going to stand up.

CHARLIE: Don't do that! If you stand up, you'll fall.

DAVE: No, I won't.

CHARLIE: Yes, you will. Sit down!

2

CHARLIE: I'm going to go faster.

DAVE: Don't do that! If you go faster, we won't see anything.

CHARLIE: Yes, we will.

DAVE: No, we won't. Slow down!

3

DAVE: I'm going to stand on this branch.

CHARLIE: Don't do that! If you stand on that branch, it'll break.

DAVE: No, it won't.

CHARLIE: Yes, it will. Come down!

4

CHARLIE: I'm going to take a photo of you.

DAVE: Don't do that! If you take a photo now, I'll look stupid.

CHARLIE: Yes, I know you will. It'll be a great photo!

Questions

What will happen if Dave stands up?
If he stands up, he'll fall.

Now answer these questions in the same way:
What will happen if Charlie goes faster?
What will happen if Dave stands on the branch?

What will happen if Charlie takes a photo now?

If Dave stands up, will he fall?
Yes, he will.

... ask and answer more questions like this.

Practice

1. What will happen?

Miss Smart wants to wear that hat.
Tell her: ... look stupid.
If you wear that hat, you'll look stupid.

1

2

Charlie wants to eat all that spaghetti.
Tell him: ... be ill.

3

Rosie wants to take another cup.
Tell her: ... drop them.

4

Arthur wants to sit on that chair.
Tell him: ... break the records.

5
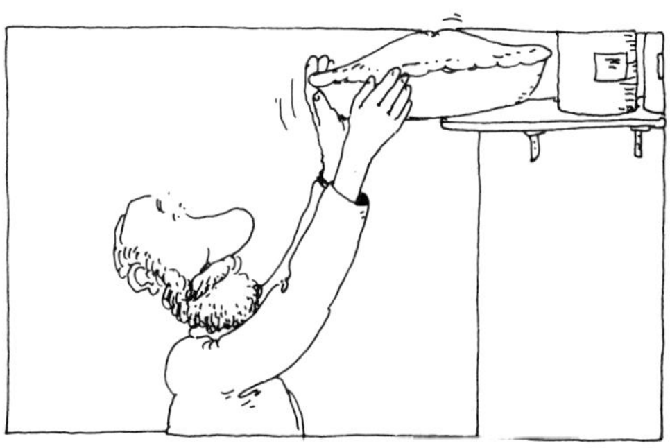

Uncle Bob wants to put the pie on the shelf.
Tell him: ... fall.

2. *Ask and answer:*

What will you do at the weekend if	**it's hot?** **it's cold?** **it rains?** **it's sunny?**

Example: A: What will you do at the weekend if it's sunny?
B: If it's sunny, I'll probably go to my uncle's farm.

Two carrot soups, please.

It's lunch-time. Pam and Charlie are in a new restaurant in Brighton.

1

PAM: Sit down, Charlie. What's the matter?

CHARLIE: Are you sure this is a good restaurant? Everyone looks ill!

PAM: Sssh! The waiter will hear you.

2

WAITER: Yes? What will you have?

PAM: I'll have carrot soup, please.

CHARLIE: And I'll have steak and chips.

PAM: But this is a vegetarian restaurant, Charlie. There isn't any meat. Er... two carrot soups, please, and some bread.

WAITER: Certainly, madam.

3

WAITER: Can you see that notice, sir?

PAM: Your cigarette, Charlie! You mustn't smoke.

WAITER: No smoking, sir.

CHARLIE: Oh yes. All right. I won't smoke.

4

WAITER: Oh... and is that your motorbike outside?

CHARLIE: Yes, it is.

WAITER: You mustn't leave it there, sir. Look at the notice. No parking!

CHARLIE: Don't worry. I'll move it now. Come on, Pam. Let's go!

19

In a hundred years

In a hundred years, there'll be fifteen thousand million people in the world. Where will they all live? Our towns will be too small for everyone. So people will live under the sea, or in the air in enormous balloons. The "houses" will be smaller than ours. And they probably won't have any windows, because there'll be nothing to see outside! Where will everyone work? There'll be a lot of factories, but they'll be full of machines. What will our food be like? What will people eat and drink? We can't be sure. The world will certainly need a lot more food, and it probably won't taste as good as food today. Perhaps things will be better in a hundred years. But we'll never know. We won't be here.

1. How many people will there be in a hundred years?
2. Why won't everyone live in towns?
3. Where will people live?
4. Will the "houses" be as big as ours?
5. Why won't the houses have any windows?
6. Will there be a lot of people in the factories?
7. Why will the world need more food in the future?
8. Will it taste better than food today?
9. Will you be here in a hundred years?

What shall we do?

CHAPTER **20**

shall I/we...?

1

Jenny and Mike are driving home. They're fifteen miles from Brighton, and they've got a flat tyre.

MIKE: Oh no! We've got a flat tyre.

JENNY: What shall we do?

MIKE: I'll change the wheel. Don't worry. It'll only take a minute.

2

MIKE: Oh no! This tyre's flat too.

JENNY: Shall we catch a bus?

MIKE: No, there won't be any buses now. It's nearly midnight.

3

JENNY: Well, shall we walk home?

MIKE: No, it'll take us hours. We're fifteen miles from Brighton.

4

JENNY: Perhaps someone'll give us a lift.

MIKE: No, there won't be another car for hours.

5

JENNY: Well, shall I go to that farm over there? Perhaps I can telephone a garage.

MIKE: Yes, that's a good idea. It'll only take you ten minutes. I'll wait here.

Questions

How long will it take Mike to change the wheel?

Why can't Mike and Jenny catch a bus?

Why can't they walk home?

Do you think anyone will give them a lift?

How long will it take Jenny to go to the farm?

What will Mike do?

Practice

1. How long will it take?

Sergeant Salt wants to visit his mother. He can go by bicycle, by plane, by boat (on the river), by car or by train.

Example: If he goes by car, he'll leave at half past eight and he'll arrive at two o'clock. So it'll take him five and a half hours.

	leave	arrive
Bicycle	4.00	24.00
Plane	9.15	9.45
Boat	9.00	16.00
Car	8.30	14.00
Train	8.15	12.45

Ask and answer:

How long will it take him if he goes by	**bicycle?** **plane?** **boat?** **car?** **train?**

2. *Practise these two dialogues:*

A: Shall we go to England next summer?
B: Yes, that's a good idea.

A: Shall we go to the country on my motorbike next weekend?
B: I'm sorry. I can't. It's my birthday on Saturday, and I'm going out with my parents.

Now work in pairs and make two similar dialogues.

It's a lot whiter!

Mrs Carter and Rosie are at home. There's a man at the door.

1

MAN: Good morning, madam. I've got some wonderful news for you.

Mrs CARTER: I'm sorry, but I'm very busy.

MAN: Don't worry, madam. I won't be long. It'll only take a minute.

2

ROSIE: What are you selling?

MAN: I'm not selling anything, young lady. I'm going to give you a packet of our new washing-powder.

Mrs CARTER: Oh, I don't want any washing-powder, thank you.

3

MAN: But if you use our powder, your washing will be as white as this shirt. Look! Incredible, isn't it?

ROSIE: Our washing's whiter than that.

Mrs CARTER: Yes, my daughter's right. Now you must excuse me. I really am very busy.

MAN: Wait a minute, madam. Why don't you show me your washing?

Mrs CARTER: All right. I will.

4

Mrs CARTER: Here you are. Look at this shirt.

MAN: Oh! It's a lot whiter than mine, isn't it?

ROSIE: Shall I give him a packet of our powder, Mum?

Some interesting news

3 Clifton Road,
Dublin.
April 9th.

Dear Bob,

How are you? You'll probably be surprised to have a letter from your old friend. I'm sorry I don't write to you very often, but now I've got some interesting news for you. I'm in Ireland at the moment. I'm coming to England on the 22nd and, if all goes well, I'll be in Brighton on the 25th. I want to talk to you about something. What are you doing next winter? I'm going to sail to Australia in my boat. It'll be quite difficult and I think I'll need some help. So I'm looking for another good sailor. Why don't you come with me? It'll take about eight months. The boat will be ready towards the end of September. So, if we leave at the beginning of October, we'll be in Australia next June. Do you want to come? Think about it. I'll see you on the 25th.

Best wishes,
Patrick.

1. Who's the letter from?
2. Why's Patrick writing to Uncle Bob?
3. Where's Patrick at the moment?
4. When's he coming to England?
5. When will he be in Brighton?
6. What's he going to do next winter?
7. Why will he need some help?
8. What's Patrick looking for?
9. When will the boat be ready?
10. How long will it take to go to Australia?
11. So when will they be in Australia?

How much is that one?

CHAPTER **21**

the one, the ones
this one, that one

1

It's Mrs Carter's birthday next week, and Mr Carter wants to buy her a present. He's looking at some rings.

GIRL: Which ring do you like, sir?

Mr CARTER: I like the one in the corner. How much is it?

GIRL: That one's five hundred pounds, sir.

Mr CARTER: Oh!

2

Mr CARTER: Have you got any watches?

GIRL: Yes, sir. Look at the ones in this box.

Mr CARTER: How much are they?

GIRL: The silver one's seventy pounds, and the gold one's ninety pounds.

Mr CARTER: Oh!

3

Mr CARTER: Have you got any lighters?

GIRL: Yes, sir. Look at the ones on the shelf.

Mr CARTER: How much are they?

GIRL: The silver ones are thirty pounds, and the gold ones are fifty pounds.

Mr CARTER: Oh!

4

Mr CARTER: I like this one. And it must be quite cheap. It's only plastic.

GIRL: Er... that one isn't for sale, sir. That one's mine.

Questions

Which ring does Mr Carter like?
Which watch is seventy pounds?
Which one is ninety pounds?
Which lighters are thirty pounds?
Which ones are fifty pounds?
Which lighter does Mr Carter like?

Practice

1. Now imagine you're in a shop and you're looking at
a) some watches, rings, etc.
b) some clothes.
Work in pairs and write a short dialogue between the shop-assistant and the customer. Then act the dialogue in front of the class; use your friends' watches, rings, clothes, etc.

2. Collect a lot of things from your friends, then ask and answer questions like these:

Example: A: Look at these pens. Which one's yours?
B: Mine's the red plastic one. (Mine's the one in your left hand/the one on the desk, etc.)

3. Spelling. *Look at these two sentences:*

a) I'm going to work for three and a half hours.
b) That one isn't yours. It's ours.

We say "hours" *and* "ours" *in the same way. Now complete these sentences using other pairs.*

1. *a*) Are you going to ... her a present?
   b) It'll take a long time if you go ... bus.
2. *a*) Shall we ... "Big Fish" next weekend?
   b) Uncle Bob likes the ... very much.
3. *a*) Be quiet! I can't ... the radio.
   b) You can leave it .... Give it to me.
4. *a*) Mike and Jenny are leaving. Give them ... coats.
   b) Put it over ..., in the corner.
5. *a*) Dave's English, and Pam's English ....
   b) I'll give you one of my bicycles. I've got....
6. *a*) Do you ... Mr Newton? He's a Member of Parliament.
   b) "Does Mike speak French?" "..., he doesn't."
7. *a*) What's the referee waiting ...?
   b) "How many do you want?" "I'll have..., please."
8. *a*) "He looks ill." "Yes, you're .... Let's telephone the doctor."
   b) I'm going to ... a letter to the manager.

Congratulations!

It's eight o'clock in the morning. Dave's got a letter. It's from the local newspaper.

1

DAVE: Look! A cheque for a hundred pounds!

Mrs CARTER: A hundred pounds!

DAVE: Yes! Listen! "Dear Sir, We are very pleased to tell you that you are the winner of our Photographic Competition this year."

Mrs CARTER: Dave! That's wonderful. Congratulations!

2

DAVE: A hundred pounds for my photo!

PAM: Which one?

ROSIE: It must be the one of me. That one's great!

DAVE: Sorry, Rosie. It's the one of the supermarket on fire.

3

Mr CARTER: Well, what are you going to do with the money, Dave?

PAM: I need some new jeans.

ROSIE: And I want a new bike, and a record-player, and a piano too!

DAVE: Hey! Wait a minute! There won't be anything for me.

Mr CARTER: Quick, Dave! Take a photo of the money. It'll be a nice souvenir!

Can you tell me the way?

21

Look at the map and imagine that you're outside the supermarket, the station, the chemist's, etc., and ask someone the way to the park, the car park, Grove School, etc.

Example: A's outside the supermarket. He wants to go to the station. He doesn't know where it is, so he's asking B.

A: Excuse me. Can you tell me the way to the station?
B: Yes, certainly. Turn left at the end of the road. Go along Queen Street. Then turn right and go along Park Street. The station's on the left.

Ian Ball

You can sail on the sea.

An English weekend

You can sit in the sun, but don't forget your umbrella!

Rosemary Drayson

You can take a boat on the river.

F. Anderson

R. P. Hoare

You can work in the garden.

... or you can get up late, then read the newspapers, and with three pints of milk, you can drink cups of tea all day.

A. D. Brunell

Revision 3

Tell me about your future, Mr Bix!

Imagine you're talking to Joe Bix, the boxer. You're asking him questions about his future, for example:

— When's your next fight?
— Who are you going to fight?
— Do you think you're as good as him?
— Do you think it'll be an easy or a difficult match?
— Do you think you'll win?

Now work in pairs. Find Joe's answers and write a dialogue; read your dialogue to the class.

Stress exercise

Say these words with the correct stress.
Example: bicycle: bicycle

1. furniture
2. tomorrow
3. manager
4. America
5. salary
6. comfortable
7. wonderful
8. inspector
9. information
10. living-room
11. sunglasses
12. probably

Dialogue invention

Look again at the dialogue on page 94. Now imagine there's a man at your door. He wants to sell you some books. You're very busy, and you don't want to buy any books. Work in pairs and write a dialogue, and act it in front of the class.

Crossword

Down

1. I can hear the bell. There's someone at the ... .
2. That's ours. Give it to ... .
3. Oh dear! I'll need a ladder. It's on the ... shelf.
4. "What does Uncle Bob ... in his junk shop?" "Everything!"
8. Can I have ... apple, please?
10. Who are they talking ...?
12. "Where's the manager?" "I don't ... ."
14. You can't sit there! That's my ... .
15. "How ... are you?" "I'm ninety-nine."
17. You must ... careful.

Across

5. He's got seventy ... on his farm.
6. The shops aren't ... on Sunday.
7. I'll have some ... and butter with my soup, please.
9. Pam, Dave, Charlie, Miss Smart and Sergeant Salt ... live in Brighton.
11. What a nice day! The ...'s blue and it's hot and sunny.
13. Mike and Jenny live in a flat but they're looking for a ... .
16. Shall we go to the swimming-... at the weekend?
17. Bob's ... is called "Sunlight".

Why don't you come?

Chorus

I'm going to leave the town
And live in the country.
I'm going to leave the town.
Why don't you come with me?
Why don't you come with me?

Let's run as fast as we can.
Let's leave the smoke and rain.
If we run as fast as we can,
We'll see the sun again.

Chorus

Shall we put the wind in our sails?
Do you want to sail with me?
If we put the wind in our sails,
We'll sail on a silver sea.

Chorus

Let's walk a thousand miles.
We've got a lot of things to find.
If we walk a thousand miles,
We'll leave the cold behind.

Chorus

Let's take the world in our hands.
Let's hold the trees and sky.
Let's take the world in our hands.
We can hold the world if we try.

There isn't much room!

CHAPTER **22**

much, many, a lot of

1

It's Saturday morning. Uncle Bob's friend, Patrick, is arriving in Brighton this evening. So Uncle Bob and Charlie are going to have a party.

There aren't many chairs in the living-room. So Charlie's making some cushions for the party.

2

There isn't much food in the kitchen, and there isn't much to drink. So Uncle Bob's buying some food and some drinks at the supermarket.

3

It's Saturday evening.

There isn't much room at the party! There are a lot of people and a lot of cushions.

4

There aren't many plates, but there's a lot to eat.

5

There aren't many glasses, but there's a lot to drink. So everyone's happy.

Questions

Are there many chairs in the living-room?
Is there much food in the kitchen?
Is there much to drink?

... ask and answer more questions like these.

Practice

1. *Find the right verb and ask and answer:*

Do you	**...**	**much** **many**	**sugar in your coffee?** **work at home?** **fish?** **tea?** **English people?** **books?** **letters?**

Examples: A: Do you have much sugar in your coffee?
B: Yes, I have a lot of sugar. I have four lumps.
A: Do you drink much tea?
B: No, I don't. I never drink tea.

2. *Practise this dialogue:*

Example: A: How much money have you got in your pocket?
B: I've got two pounds.
A: Really? I've only got thirty pence.

Now work in pairs and make another dialogue with "How much / how many" *and words like* "brothers, sisters, records, etc.".

3. Pronunciation. *Listen first, and then repeat:*

Thin Bill Hill and his pretty sister Linda have got a fish and chip shop in Brighton. Bill's shop's big and his chips are cheap, so Bill and Linda are always busy. Bill Hill's very quick. He can fill fifty big bags with chips in six minutes.

Now look at these pairs of words. Say the words and then complete the sentences.

a) live, leave
1. Where do you...? 2. He's going to ... Spain.

b) chip, cheap
1. Those glasses are ..., aren't they? 2. Have a ... .

c) sit, seat
1. Is this anyone's ...? 2. Where shall we ...?

I don't want much, thank you.

Pam's in the kitchen. She's cooking the breakfast. The Carters are having sausages, eggs, bacon and tomatoes this morning.

1

PAM: Breakfast's ready. Come on, everyone. It'll get cold.

Mr CARTER: I don't want much, thank you, Pam. No sausages for me.

PAM: Why not? What's the matter with them?

Mr CARTER: Nothing, dear. They look delicious. But I think I'm getting too fat.

2

PAM: Well, one sausage won't make you fat, Dad.

Mr CARTER: Oh, all right. Perhaps I'll have one. But don't give me many tomatoes, just one or two.

3

ROSIE: Tea, everyone?

Mr CARTER: No sugar for me thanks, Rosie.

ROSIE: But you always have sugar, Dad.

Mr CARTER: Oh, all right. But don't give me much. Just one lump.

4

DAVE: How many pieces of toast do you want, Dad?

Mr CARTER: Oh, er... I'll just have one piece, Dave. And I mustn't eat much at lunch-time.

Mrs CARTER: All right, dear. Just chicken pie and potatoes?

22

He won't see much!

Next month Charlie's going on holiday. He's going to go round Scotland on his motorbike. He won't need much money because he's going to sleep in his tent, and he isn't going to eat in expensive restaurants. He can't take many things with him, because there won't be much room on his motorbike. He's just taking a tent, a camping-gas, a cup, a plate, a knife and fork, and a map. He's leaving Brighton on Saturday, June the fifth, and he's coming home on Sunday, June the thirteenth. Charlie doesn't know Scotland and he wants to see everything. But it'll take two days to go to Scotland and two days to come home. So he'll only be there for five days. He won't see much in five days, will he?

1. When's Charlie going on holiday?
2. What's he going to do?
3. Will he need much money? Why not?
4. Can he take many things with him? Why not?
5. What's he taking?
6. When's he leaving Brighton?
7. When's he coming home?
8. What does Charlie want to see?
9. How long will he be in Scotland?
10. Why will he only be there for five days?
11. Will he see much?

There was a terrible storm

CHAPTER **23**

was, were

1

Last Monday night there was a terrible storm in Brighton. Arthur was very frightened.

On Tuesday morning he wasn't in his basket. He was in the cupboard!

2

Pam was in bed, but it was difficult to sleep.

So in the morning she was very tired. She wasn't very nice to her customers.

3

Dave's new shoes were outside. They were in the garden.

So in the morning they were full of water. Mr and Mrs Carter weren't very pleased.

4

On Monday night the boats were on the beach.

But they weren't there on Tuesday morning. Sergeant Salt was very surprised, because the boats were in the car park!

Questions

Was there a storm in Brighton last Monday?
Yes, there was.

Was Arthur frightened?
Yes, he was.

Was he in his basket on Tuesday morning?
No, he wasn't.

... ask and answer more questions like these.

Were Dave's shoes outside?
Yes, they were.

Were Mr and Mrs Carter pleased?
No, they weren't.

... ask and answer more questions like these.

Why was Arthur frightened?
Why wasn't Pam nice to her customers?
Why weren't Mr and Mrs Carter pleased?
Why was Sergeant Salt surprised?

Practice

1. Do you remember Jack, Mike and Jenny's neighbour? It was his birthday yesterday and, last night, he had a party. Mike and Jenny weren't there. They were in bed. But there was a lot of noise, and it was difficult to sleep. So this morning they're very tired. Jenny's talking to a friend at work. Can you complete their conversation?

Friend: What's the matter, Jenny? You look very tired.
Jenny:
Friend: Oh, I see. Was it a good party?
Jenny:
Friend: What do you mean? You were there, weren't you?
Jenny:
Friend: Why are you tired then?
Jenny:
Friend: Poor Jenny!

2. *Ask and answer:*

Where were you	**at midnight last night?** **at half past seven this morning?** **last Saturday afternoon?** **yesterday morning?** **last August?**

Were you on television last night?

It's Saturday night. Mike and Jenny are in a pub called the Red Lion.

1

JENNY: Hey, Mike. Look at that man.

MIKE: Which man?

JENNY: The one with the red shirt. He's an actor, isn't he?

MIKE: No. Don't be silly.

2

JENNY: But he was on television last night. He was in that awful film.

MIKE: No, he wasn't. He's much smaller than the man in the film.

JENNY: Well, people look bigger on television. I'm sure it's him. I'm going to ask him.

3

JENNY: Excuse me. Were you on television last night?

ACTOR: Yes, I was. It was an awful film, wasn't it?

JENNY: No, it wasn't. It was very good. You were wonderful.

ACTOR: Really? Oh, thank you. Can I buy you a drink?

4

JENNY: Oh... er, I'm with my husband. He thinks you're a wonderful actor!

ACTOR: Oh, thank you very much. Well, why don't you call him? I'll buy him a drink too.

23

It was only a film

Earlier this evening Dave was at the cinema. It was a science fiction film and it was very good. Four men were in a boat on the sea, and there was an awful storm. They were frightened because they were five miles from the beach and there wasn't a radio in the boat. And that wasn't all. Just behind the boat, there was an enormous fish with terrible, silver teeth...

Dave's in bed now. He's asleep and he's dreaming. His bed's an enormous fish. Dave's fighting but the fish is stronger than him. The blankets on his bed are getting heavier and heavier. The fish is pulling him under the water. He can't see anything. Aaagh!... Dave's awake now. He's looking for the light switch. "It was only a dream. I think it was only a dream. Where's the light switch?"

1. Where was Dave earlier this evening?
2. What was the film like?
3. Where were the four men?
4. Why were they frightened?
5. Where's Dave now?
6. What's he doing?
7. What's Dave doing in his dream?
8. Is he as strong as the fish?
9. What's happening to the blankets?
10. What's the fish doing?
11. Dave's awake now. What's he looking for?
12. Can he find the light switch?

What did he do in Scotland?

CHAPTER **24**

simple past: regular verbs

1

Last week Charlie was on holiday in Scotland. One day it was very cold, and it rained all day.

In the evening Charlie stopped near a farm. There was a big tree near the road. It was dry under the tree, so he decided to put his tent there.

2

The next morning Charlie was cold and hungry, so he cooked a big breakfast in his tent.

Then someone walked round the tent. Charlie didn't move. He listened and waited.

3

Nothing happened, so he looked outside. It was the farmer. He didn't look very friendly. He shouted at Charlie and showed him a notice on the gate: "No camping".

4

Charlie didn't want to leave. He wanted to finish his egg and bacon. So he offered the farmer some breakfast.

It was a good idea. The farmer invited him to stay all week!

Questions

Where was Charlie last week?
What was the weather like?
Where did Charlie stop?
What did he decide to do?
Why did he cook a big breakfast?
When someone walked round the tent, what did Charlie do?

Did the farmer look friendly?
No, he didn't.

Did he shout at Charlie?
Yes, he did.

... ask and answer more questions like these.

Practice

1. *Ask and answer:*

What time **When**	**did**	**you arrive home last night?** **you arrive at school this morning?** **your last lesson finish?** **the English lesson start?**

Example: A: When did you arrive home last night?
B: I arrived home at quarter past six.

2. *Now practise the short answers.*

ask

Did you	**watch television last night?** **come to school by bus this morning?** **listen to the radio this morning?** **make your bed this morning?** **do the washing-up yesterday?**

answer **Yes, I did.** or **No, I didn't.**

Charlie wasn't there

Pam was at a party this evening. It's one o'clock in the morning. She's at home now. Rosie's waiting for her.

1

ROSIE: Hello, Pam. You're late. Was it a good party?

PAM: Not bad. Why aren't you in bed?

ROSIE: I decided to wait for you. Did you see anyone interesting?

PAM: Don't be silly, Rosie. Go to bed.

ROSIE: Well, did you talk to anyone?

PAM: Of course I did. Don't ask silly questions.

2

ROSIE: Well, why do you look so miserable then?

PAM: I'm not miserable. I'm tired, that's all.

ROSIE: Did you dance with a lot of boys?

PAM: No, I didn't dance with anyone.

ROSIE: Why not?

PAM: Because I didn't want to dance.

3

PAM: Why are you laughing? I don't think it's funny.

ROSIE: I'm not laughing. Was Charlie there, Pam?

PAM: No, he wasn't. Goodnight!

24

They talked about the past

Last night Uncle Bob and his friend Patrick talked about their past. Charlie listened to them for six hours! Uncle Bob showed them all his old photos. There was one of Uncle Bob when he was twenty, with his first beard. There was another one of Patrick and Uncle Bob at a party. They were with two very pretty girls. Charlie looked at it and laughed. But Bob and Patrick looked very miserable. So Charlie opened a bottle of whisky. There were a lot of photos of boats too. There was a problem with one of the photos. Uncle Bob was sure the boat was called "The Sailor's Dream" and Patrick was sure it was called "The Dreaming Sailor". Bob shouted at Patrick. Patrick jumped out of his chair and shouted at Bob. So Charlie opened another bottle of whisky.
At two o'clock in the morning they were all asleep in their chairs. There were a lot of old photos on the floor, and two empty bottles on the table.

1. What did Charlie, Uncle Bob and Patrick do last night?
2. What did Uncle Bob show them?
3. When did Uncle Bob have his first beard?
4. What were the two girls in the photo like?
5. Did Charlie think the photo was funny?
6. Do you think Bob and Patrick wanted to be young again? How do you know this?
7. What did Charlie do?
8. Why did Bob shout at Patrick?
9. Why did Patrick shout at Bob?
10. So what did Charlie do?
11. Where were they at two o'clock?
12. Was there any whisky in the bottles?

I had it this morning

CHAPTER **25**

simple past:
irregular verbs

1

It's two o'clock in the afternoon. Uncle Bob's looking for his pipe.

UNCLE BOB: That's funny! I can't find my pipe. I'm sure I had it this morning.

2

What did I do this morning?
I got up, and I went into the kitchen.

3

I made a cup of tea, and I took my pipe out of my pocket.

4

But I didn't smoke it, because then the postman came.
So I put it on the table, and went to the door.

5

CHARLIE: Hello, Uncle Bob. Look, I found your pipe in the garden this morning. Arthur had it. Perhaps he thought it was a bone.

UNCLE BOB: No, he's more intelligent than that. He thinks I smoke too much!

Questions

Did Uncle Bob have his pipe this morning?
What did he do this morning?
Where did he go?
Did he smoke his pipe?

... ask and answer more questions like these.

Practice

1. *Ask and answer:*

What did you do	**yesterday?** **last Saturday evening?** **at the weekend?** **last summer?**

Example: A: What did you do last Saturday evening?
B: I went to the cinema.
A: Really? What did you see?
B: I saw a film called "The Politician". It wasn't very good. In fact, it was awful.

2. Imagine you had a camping holiday last year. Write a letter to a friend, and tell him/her about your holiday. Where did you go? Who did you go with? What was the weather like? Were there many people there, or was it very quiet? How long did you stay? What did you do? Begin your letter "Dear...", and finish "Love from..." or "Best wishes, ...".

3. Pronunciation. *Listen first, and then repeat:*

Jack Bat lived in a flat and worked in a hat factory.
Jack had a fat, black cat called Max.
The mad man had a hammer and a black plastic bag in his hand.

Now look at these pairs of words. Say the words and then complete the sentences.

a) cat, cut
1. Here's a knife. ... the bread. 2. He's got a ... and a dog.

b) match, much
1. Let's watch the .... 2. Have you got ...?

c) ran, run
1. Don't ...! I'm tired. 2. He ... out of the house.

The electric blanket

There was a sale at one of the big shops in Brighton last week. Miss Smart bought an electric blanket. Now she wants to change it, so she's talking to the shop-assistant.

1

Miss SMART: I bought this electric blanket here last week. I want to change it, please.

ASSISTANT: What's the matter with it, madam?

Miss SMART: It's too big.

ASSISTANT: Too big?

Miss SMART: Yes. I wanted one for a single bed. You gave me one for a double bed.

ASSISTANT: Oh, I see.

2

ASSISTANT: You didn't buy it in the sale, did you, madam?

Miss SMART: Yes, I did.

ASSISTANT: Oh. Well, I can't change it then.

Miss SMART: But it was your mistake, not mine. What am I going to do with it?

3

ASSISTANT: Er... well, why don't you put half the blanket under you and the other half . . . er. . . over you?

Miss SMART: Like a sausage in a sandwich, you mean?

ASSISTANT: Yes, yes. Oh, very funny, madam, very funny.

4

Miss SMART: I don't think it's funny. I want a smaller blanket.

ASSISTANT: I can't give you a smaller blanket, madam. Er. . . but I can sell you a double bed.

25

Room number thirteen

Last week the White Tree Hotel was nearly full, so Mrs Carter was very busy. One afternoon two Americans came to the hotel. They were lucky, because Mrs Carter only had one free room. She took their name and gave them the key. But then the wife said she didn't want the room, because it was number 13.
Mrs Carter had a good idea. She left the man and woman at the desk and went to the manager's office. Then the manager went upstairs and Mrs Carter went back to the desk. She said there was another free room and she offered it to the two Americans. They were very pleased and they went upstairs with her. Mrs Carter showed them their room. The number was on the door — number 12A. And so for one night at the White Tree Hotel, room 13 didn't exist!

1. Why was Mrs Carter busy last week?
2. When the two Americans came, how many free rooms did Mrs Carter have?
3. What did Mrs Carter do?
4. Why didn't the wife want to take the room?
5. Mrs Carter had a good idea, didn't she?
6. Where did she go? Then what happened?
7. What did Mrs Carter say?
8. Did the two Americans take the room?
9. What was the number on the door of their room?
10. Was the room usually number 12A?

Did you hurt yourself?

CHAPTER **26**

reflexive pronouns

1 

Sergeant Salt woke up late yesterday.

He jumped out of bed and ran to the bathroom.

2 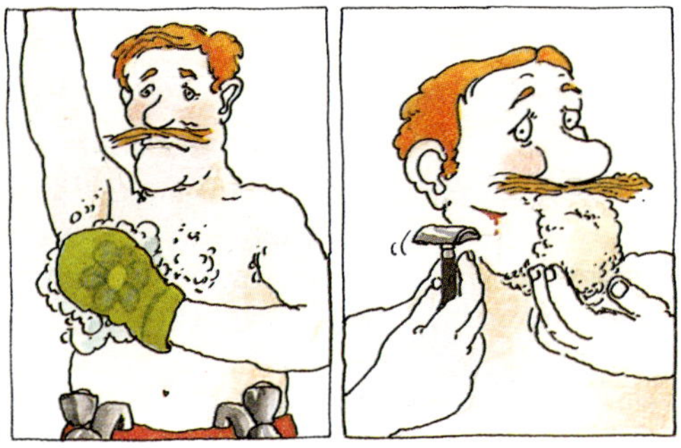

He washed, and then he shaved.

But he shaved too quickly and he cut himself.

3 

He got dressed in a hurry, and he fell and hurt himself.

4 

He made his breakfast too quickly, and he burnt himself.

5 

Then he remembered. He looked at himself in the mirror and laughed. It was Saturday, and he never works on Saturday morning.

So he went back to bed.

Questions

Imagine you're asking Sergeant Salt questions:

Why did you cut yourself, Sergeant?
I cut myself because I shaved too quickly.

Why did you hurt yourself?
Why did you burn yourself?
What did you do when you looked at yourself in the mirror?

Practice

1. *Example:* Your friend's cutting some bread, but he's looking at you.
What do you tell him?
— Be careful! You'll cut yourself!

a) Your friend's making a big fire. He's standing too near. What do you tell him?
b) Your friend's got a piece of glass in her hand. What do you tell her?
c) Your friend's trying to move a very heavy box. What do you tell him?

2. *Ask and answer:*

Do **Does**	**you** **you and your brothers and sisters** **firemen** **your mother** **your father**	**ever** **often**

talk to yourself? **look at yourself in the mirror?** **burn yourselves when you cook the dinner?** **hurt themselves when they're at work?** **burn herself when she makes the toast?** **cut himself when he shaves?**

Example: A: Do you and your brothers and sisters ever burn yourselves when you cook the dinner?
B: No, we never burn ourselves, because we never cook the dinner!

Say cheese!

Dave's got a job for the summer holidays. He's a photographer on the beach at Brighton.

1 

DAVE: Photograph, madam?

WOMAN: Yes, why not? Just a minute, dear. I must make myself pretty.

DAVE: Are you enjoying yourself in Brighton?

WOMAN: Oh, yes. I always enjoy myself here. I come every year, you know.

2 

WOMAN: There! I'm ready.

DAVE: O.K. Don't move! Say "cheese"!

WOMAN: C-h-e-e-s-e.

DAVE: That's fine. There!

WOMAN: Thank you, dear. That'll be a wonderful souvenir.

3 

WOMAN: When will the photo be ready?

DAVE: At about five, madam. Here's our address. Have a nice afternoon.

WOMAN: Thank you, dear. Goodbye.

4 

DAVE: Don't move, sir! This will be a wonderful souvenir of your holiday.

MAN: Listen! If you don't move, I'll give you a wonderful souvenir of me!

DAVE: All right, all right! I'm going. Have a nice holiday, sir!

26

Do-it-yourself!

Do you want a new home — the home of your dreams?
Well, you can have it. And you won't need much money.
You can change your home yourself in a weekend.
Visit our new "Do-it-yourself" shop at 82, High Street, Brighton.
You'll find a big selection of wallpaper and paint.
A new colour for each room!
If you need a hammer or a ladder, come to us.
If you want to make a cupboard or some shelves, we'll help you.
It isn't difficult.
And don't worry — you won't hurt yourself!
Just read our instructions and the job will be easy.
So, remember, don't stay in bed next weekend!
Paint a wall! Make some furniture! Enjoy yourself!

1. Is there a cheap way to change your home?
2. Where's the new "Do-it-yourself" shop?
3. What can you buy at the shop?
4. What can you make yourself?
5. What must you read before you start?

What were they doing?

CHAPTER 27

past continuous

1

It's half past two on Saturday afternoon. Dave and Rosie are looking for Pam.

ROSIE: Mum, where's Pam?

Mrs CARTER: I don't know, dear. But I saw her at two.

DAVE: What was she doing?

Mrs CARTER: She was going out.

2

It's three o'clock. Mr Carter's looking for his wife.

Mr CARTER: Dave, where's Mum?

DAVE: I don't know, Dad. But we saw her at half past two.

Mr CARTER: What was she doing?

ROSIE: She was painting the garage.

3

It's half past three. Pam's looking for Dave and Rosie.

PAM: Dad, where are Dave and Rosie?

Mr CARTER: I don't know, dear. But I saw them at three.

PAM: What were they doing?

Mr CARTER: They were listening to your records.

4

It's four o'clock. Dave and Rosie are looking for Pam.

ROSIE: Dad, where's Pam?

DAD: I don't know, dear. But I saw her at half past three.

DAVE: What was she doing?

Mr CARTER: She was looking for you.

Questions

What was Pam doing at two?
What was Mrs Carter doing at half past two?
What were Dave and Rosie doing at half past two?
What were they doing at three?

... ask and answer more questions like these.

What do you think Dave and Rosie were doing at half past three?

Was Mrs Carter painting the garage at half past two?
Yes, she was.

Were Dave and Rosie listening to Pam's records at three?
Yes, they were.

... ask and answer more questions like these.

Practice

1. What were you doing at ten?

Sergeant Salt's questioning six men.

Example: Sergeant: Where were you at ten last night?
Man 1: I was in a pub.
Sergeant: What were you doing?
Man 1: I was having a drink.

Now look at the other men and ask the same questions.

2. *Work in pairs and practise this dialogue:*

A: I came to your house yesterday morning, but you weren't there.
B: Yes, I was. I was in the living-room. I was watching television, so I didn't hear the bell.

Now make a similar dialogue. Change the underlined words.

Me and Arthur, of course.

Pam's having a cup of coffee with Charlie.

1

PAM: I saw your uncle this morning, Charlie. He was talking to Miss Smart again.

CHARLIE: Yes, they're very good friends at the moment.

2

PAM: But Bob's sailing to Australia soon. She isn't going with him, is she?

CHARLIE: No, of course she isn't! She's going to work in the junk shop.

PAM: Oh, that's great. I thought Bob was going to sell it.

CHARLIE: No, he doesn't want to sell anything. He'll be back one day, you know.

3

PAM: You must be quite upset, Charlie.

CHARLIE: Oh, don't worry. We'll be all right together.

PAM: We? Charlie, what do you mean?

CHARLIE: Me and Arthur, of course.

PAM: Oh yes, of course.

Why was Mr Carter late?

27

Look at the pictures and say what happened to Mr Carter yesterday. These words will help you:

1. Mr Carter / farmer   he / drive / road / cars / stop   Mr Carter's car / behind / bus   people on the bus / look at / laugh   Mr Carter / look at / watch / worried / in a hurry

2. Mr Carter / get out   cow / road   policeman / bus-driver / try to pull / rope   bus-driver / fall / hurt himself   everyone / watch / laugh

3. shop-assistant / try to move / umbrella   cow / start to eat   driver / have a cup of tea   policeman / write a report

4. Mr Carter / talk to / cow   it / decide to move   everyone / surprised   policeman / pleased   driver / get into / bus   man / take a photograph / Mr Carter / cow

Take the one I gave you

CHAPTER **28**

"who, that"
omission of "who, that"

1

Uncle Bob's leaving for Australia tomorrow. What's he going to take with him? Charlie's helping him to decide.

UNCLE BOB: I'll need a bag for all my things. Which one shall I take?

CHARLIE: Take the one that isn't full of holes. The one I gave you.

2

UNCLE BOB: I'll need a scarf. Which one shall I take?

CHARLIE: Take the one that goes with your pullover. The one you bought last week.

3

UNCLE BOB: I must take some books with me. I'll take this one.

CHARLIE: "The Seven Seas". Who wrote that one, Uncle Bob?

UNCLE BOB: Ann Henry, the girl who sailed round the world. You know, the girl we saw on T.V. last week.

4

UNCLE BOB: I must take that one too.

CHARLIE: "Don't drop the eggs". Who wrote this one?

UNCLE BOB: Bill Galley, a man who was a cook on a boat.

CHARLIE: He's the man you need on your boat, Uncle Bob.

UNCLE BOB: What do you mean, Charlie?

Questions

Which bag will Uncle Bob take?
Which scarf will he take?

Who's Ann Henry?
Who's Bill Galley?

Practice

1. Do you remember these people?

Example: He's the actor who was in the Red Lion Pub. He was in a film that was on television. He's the actor Mike and Jenny saw.

1

2

3

4

5

6

2. Pronunciation. *Listen first, and then repeat.*

Paul Porter's got a daughter called Dora. Dora isn't tall because she's only four. Paul Porter bought his daughter a ball. This morning Dora was playing with her ball on the floor near the door. Paul saw his daughter and thought: "If someone opens the door, poor Dora will fall."

Now look at these pairs of words. Say the words and then complete the sentences.

a) walk, work
1. Do you ... to school? 2. Where does he ...?

b) short, shirt
1. Is it long or ...? 2. He's wearing a green ....

Good news!

Sergeant Salt and Police Constable Potter are at the police station. Sergeant Salt's reading a letter.

1

SERG. SALT: I've got a very interesting letter here, Constable Potter.

P.C. POTTER: Oh dear. What does she say, Sergeant?

SERG. SALT: She? What do you mean?

P.C. POTTER: Oh ... er... my wife said she was going to write to you, Sergeant.

SERG. SALT: Really?

P.C. POTTER: Yes. You see, she doesn't like the job I've got. She says we need more money.

2

SERG. SALT: Well, the letter I'm reading isn't from your wife.

P.C. POTTER: Oh, I'm very pleased, Sergeant.

SERG. SALT: No, Constable Potter. I've got some very good news for you. You're a sergeant!

P.C. POTTER: A sergeant, Sergeant! Good heavens! That'll be a surprise for my wife.

3

SERG. SALT: And that isn't all, Sergeant Potter. The person who wrote this letter remembered me too.

P.C. POTTER: Really, Sergeant?

SERG. SALT: Inspector, Sergeant Potter! You're talking to Inspector Salt!

P.C. POTTER: Congratulations, Sergeant... I mean, Inspector!

Bon Voyage!

Yesterday was a big day for Bob Kipper and Patrick O'Hara. They left Brighton yesterday morning in their boat "Sea Dog". They're going to sail to Australia, and it'll take them about eight months. The two men are very good sailors. Bob Kipper's the man who won the Brighton Regatta Race earlier this year.
"Sea Dog" is a big, comfortable boat. There's a lot of room, and the two men have got everything they need: food and water, books and maps, a cooker and a radio. All their friends came to say goodbye. Mr Philip Carter, the Brighton vet, came with his family. Charlie Kipper was there with Arthur, his uncle's dog. Arthur's staying in Brighton, and he looked quite upset! Mr Richard Newton, the local Member of Parliament, offered everyone champagne. Then, at ten o'clock, "Sea Dog" left for Australia. From everyone in Brighton: Goodbye! Good luck! And bon voyage!

1. What happened yesterday morning?
2. How long will it take to go to Australia?
3. What did Bob Kipper win earlier this year?
4. What's "Sea Dog" like?
5. What are Bob and Patrick taking with them?
6. Who came to say goodbye to Bob and Patrick?
7. Why did Arthur look upset?
8. What did Mr Newton do?
9. What time did "Sea Dog" leave?

Martin

Yes, this is London, not Tokyo!

English faces and places

« Excuse me, Constable, where did you find that incredible moustache ? »

Martin

A cricket match. If you don't play cricket, you'll never understand it!

Martin

In the country — a farm in Kent.

Martin

Martin

« A pint, please ! »
An English pub — the answer
to everyone's problems.

If you want to buy a house, then go to Mr Evans, the estate agent.

Martin

Revision 4

Pronunciation

Put the words with the same sound together (two groups for each number):

1. thin, cheese, pretty, busy, meat, chip, live, piece, dream, free, guitar, leave.

2. talk, girl, short, door, hurt, shirt, saw, turn, more, work, first, storm.

3. boot, put, roof, blue, pull, cook, shoe, food, look, soup, foot, good.

Composition exercise

Imagine you're Mr Newton, the politician. You're writing a chapter of your autobiography; it's called "When I was young". Write a short passage; the answers to these questions will help you:
Where did you live when you were young? What was your house like? Did you have any brothers or sisters? What was your school like? Did you enjoy yourself at school? When did you leave school? What did you do? When did you decide you wanted to be a politician?

Stress exercise

Say these words with the correct stress. *Example:* announcement: announcement. Then make a sentence with each word.

1. Australia
2. surgery
3. remember
4. photographer
5. newspaper
6. swimming-pool
7. policeman
8. supermarket
9. mechanic
10. intelligent
11. customer
12. incredible

Dialogue invention

Look at the dialogue between Miss Smart and the shop-assistant on page 118. Now imagine that last week you bought a T-shirt in a local shop. You wanted a yellow one but the assistant gave you a pink one. Now you want to change it because it doesn't go with your trousers. But the assistant says he/she can't change it because you bought it in a sale. Work in pairs and write the dialogue between you and the assistant, and then act the dialogue.

Dialogue completion

This morning you found a purse near your house, so you took it to the police station in town. Can you complete the conversation between you and the policeman?

Policeman: Where did you find the wallet?
You:
Policeman: And when did you find it?
You:
Policeman: Was there any money in the wallet when you found it?
You:
Policeman: Well, that's very funny! It's empty now. Where's the ten pence?
You:
Policeman: You took it!!
You:
Policeman: All right, you didn't have any money, but that ten pence wasn't yours.
You:
Policeman: What do you mean "in a hurry"?
You:
Policeman: Oh, I see! You came here by bus. Well, how are you going to go home?
You:
Policeman: But it'll take you about half an hour, and it's raining.
You:
Policeman: Oh, all right. Here you are!
You:
Policeman: Goodbye!

What am I?

1. If you sit on me, you'll hurt yourself. If you want to cut some meat, you'll need me.

2. I'm enormous. In fact, you don't really know where I start or where I finish. I'm sometimes blue, but not always.

3. I'm long and thin. I'm probably in a cupboard in your bedroom. You need me when it's cold and windy.

4. I look very nice on your walls, but not on your clothes. If you drink me, I'll probably make you ill.

5. I'm white. You put me in tea or coffee. You'll find me in a box. If you eat a lot of me, I'll make you fat.

The man I didn't know

Last night I stood outside my door.
I looked inside and I saw
A man I didn't know.
He was laughing, I could see,
He was laughing, laughing at me,
The man I didn't know.

Chorus

But I didn't know it was only a dream.
I didn't know it was only a dream.
Ooh, Ooh, Ooh!
A very bad dream!

I went to town. What could I do?
Everything was strange, everything was new,
With the man I didn't know.
He was waiting outside the cinema.
He was at the corner; he was in my car,
The man I didn't know.

Chorus

I telephoned a very good friend;
A strange man answered at the other end,
A man I didn't know.
I saw a mirror on a shelf,
I was very surprised. I couldn't see myself,
Just a man I didn't know.

Chorus

I shouted for help. I looked for the light.
I found myself in bed. It was nearly midnight.
Where was the man I didn't know?
I looked in the mirror on the bathroom wall.
I was older, and fatter, and very small.
I was the man I didn't know.

Final revision exercises

1. Complete these sentences with a preposition.

1. Hey, Dave, why don't you try these red trousers ...?
2. Charlie's garage is ... Park Street, isn't it?
3. I'll see you ... half past eleven then.
4. They aren't sure. They think it'll take ... a month.
5. Who are you waiting ...?
6. Sergeant Salt usually gets ... early.
7. Where's Madrid? It's ... Spain, isn't it?
8. Shall we go ... Miss Smart's employment agency?
9. Mr and Mrs Carter are ... holiday this week.
10. I can't find Arthur. Can you help me to look ... him?
11. Dave's ... school and Pam's ... work.
12. Don't decide now. Think ... it.
13. Constable Potter's standing ... front ... the police station.
14. Shall we go ... bus or ... train?
15. Good heavens! He's going to jump ... ... the window ... the car.
16. Mike waited for Jenny ... the supermarket ... twenty minutes.
17. It isn't very good; ... fact, it's awful.
18. Can I have a piece ... bread, please?
19. Is it ... the left or ... the right?
20. I'm sorry, but Mr Carter's busy ... the moment.
21. The Chinese restaurant's ... there. Look!
22. What a nice house! Is it ... sale?
23. Sergeant Salt drives ... Brighton every Saturday night.
24. Why don't you put half the blanket ... you and the other half ... you?

2. Put these words into the plural, and then make a sentence with each plural word.

1. policeman
2. secretary
3. woman
4. toothbrush
5. yourself
6. fireman
7. tomato
8. watch
9. lady
10. sandwich
11. glass
12. shelf

3. Example:
— Where did Mr and Mrs Carter go last year? (Italy)
— They went to Italy.

1. What did Mr Carter buy for Mrs Carter's birthday? (a lighter)
2. What did the porter take? (my case)
3. When did you see Patrick's boat? (last Sunday)
4. What did he have for lunch? (steak and chips)
5. Where did you put my scarf? (in the cupboard)
6. What did Uncle Bob make? (a chicken pie)
7. When did you see the fire-engines? (this morning)
8. What did he give you? (some records)
9. What time did they get up? (seven thirty)
10. Where did Charlie go? (to the pub)
11. What did Dave burn? (the toast)

4. Complete these sentences with "so, because, but" or "and".

1. He took his umbrella ... it was raining.
2. Charlie wasn't there, ... Pam went home.
3. I saw Bob, ... I didn't see Patrick.
4. Mr Hardy works at Grove School, ... Mike works there too.
5. The dog ran into the cupboard ... it was frightened.
6. There'll be a lot of people, ... we'll need a lot of glasses.

5. Put the verbs into the correct tense.

1. Please be quiet! I (listen) to the radio.
2. "Did you hear the telephone?" "No, I didn't. I (sit) in the garden."
3. Goodbye! I (see) you tomorrow at half past ten.
4. I (have) egg and chips please, waiter.
5. The Carters (live) in Brighton.
6. Mr Carter (get) fat. He (eat) a lot of potatoes.
7. If it rains tomorrow, we (go) to the cinema.
8. Rosie (go) to a party last night.
9. The train always (leave) at ten to eight.
10. Hurry up! Your breakfast (get) cold.
11. Uncle Bob (be) fifty next week.
12. I can't talk to you now. I (cook) the dinner.

6. Complete these sentences with the correct form of "to be, to have" or "have got".

1. How old ... you? I ... fifteen.
2. Sergeant Salt always ... egg and bacon for breakfast.
3. Enjoy yourself! ... a good holiday!
4. Is lunch ready? I ... hungry.
5. Dave ... a new camera.
6. Good heavens! You ... right.
7. We ... an English lesson at the moment.
8. Mr Carter ... a very interesting job.
9. What ... the weather like? It ... hot and sunny.
10. Pam ... long hair and she ... quite tall.
11. Bob and Charlie ... a party last week.
12. How tall ... you? ... you as tall as Charlie?

7. Can you complete these sentences with question-tags?

1. Miss Smart didn't think it was funny, ...
2. The shop-assistant wasn't very nice, ...
3. You won't forget, ...
4. They were watching television, ...
5. It's very foggy, ...
6. He's going to sell it, ...
7. Mr Hardy usually wins, ...
8. Mike doesn't like his neighbour, Jack, ...
9. Mr Carter can't play the guitar, ...
10. They've got a lot of old junk, ...
11. She took the exam yesterday, ...
12. He'll slow down if you ask him, ...

8. Make sentences with "how much" or "how many".

Example:
records / he / four
— How many records has he got?
— He's only got four.

1. fingers / he / four
2. furniture / she / a bed and a table
3. teeth / he / two
4. bread / you / one piece
5. sugar / they / two lumps
6. matches / we / three

9. Write these sentences again: use contractions.

Example:

He has got a ladder.

He's got a ladder.

1. That man is the manager of the factory.
2. Mrs Carter is standing at the bus-stop.
3. I have not got much whisky.
4. Slow down! You must not drive quickly when you are in town.
5. Dave has got a knife but he has not got a fork.
6. Do not worry! He will not be late.
7. They did not have a very good holiday.
8. I am going to paint the walls of my bedroom.
9. I will buy some ice-creams.
10. There is a policeman in our garden.
11. We need a hammer. I will ask Mrs Carter. She has got one.
12. I do not think it is a very good match.

10. The following sentences are all answers to questions. Can you find the questions?

1. They were eating their breakfast.
2. It's Constable Potter's.
3. He's quite tall. He's got brown hair and a beard.
4. She left at eight o'clock this morning.
5. Because I need a new toothbrush.
6. Over there, on the corner of the street.

11. Answer these questions with short answers ("Yes, I do. No, I won't." etc.).

1. Do you speak English?
2. Will you be at home this evening?
3. Were you asleep at midnight last night?
4. Do you drink much whisky?
5. Do you live in the country?
6. Did you have a nice weekend?
7. Are you going out tomorrow night?
8. Will you be at school tomorrow?
9. Did you eat anything for breakfast this morning?
10. Are you wearing jeans at the moment?
11. Have you got brown hair?
12. Are you going to do the next exercise?

12. Answer these questions about the people in the book.

1. What's Charlie's job?
2. Where does Pam work?
3. Where do Mike and Jenny live?
4. Describe Miss Smart. What's she like?
5. Who always sings in the bath?
6. What are Uncle Bob and Patrick going to do at the end of the book?
7. How many daughters have Mr and Mrs Carter got?
8. Can Rosie play the guitar?
9. Why did Pam got to Miss Smart's employment agency?
10. Where does Mrs Carter work?
11. What does Sergeant Salt usually do on Saturday night?
12. Who won the Brighton Regatta this year?

Numbers

		10	ten	20	twenty	30	thirty
1	one	11	eleven	21	twenty-one	40	forty
2	two	12	twelve	22	twenty-two	50	fifty
3	three	13	thirteen	23	twenty-three	60	sixty
4	four	14	fourteen	24	twenty-four	70	seventy
5	five	15	fifteen	25	twenty-five	80	eighty
6	six	16	sixteen	26	twenty-six	90	ninety
7	seven	17	seventeen	27	twenty-seven		
8	eight	18	eighteen	28	twenty-eight		
9	nine	19	nineteen	29	twenty-nine		

100	a hundred
101	a hundred and one
102	a hundred and two
200	two hundred
300	three hundred
400	four hundred
500	five hundred
600	six hundred
700	seven hundred
800	eight hundred
900	nine hundred
1,000	a thousand
1,001	a thousand and one
1,100	one thousand one hundred
1,200	one thousand two hundred

2,000	two thousand
3,000	three thousand
4,000	four thousand
5,000	five thousand
6,000	six thousand
7,000	seven thousand
8,000	eight thousand
9,000	nine thousand
10,000	ten thousand
100,000	a hundred thousand
1,000,000	a million
1,100,000	one million, one hundred thousand
1,220,222	one million, two hundred and twenty thousand, two hundred and twenty-two.

		10th	tenth	20th	twentieth	30th	thirtieth
1st	first	11th	eleventh	21st	twenty-first	40th	fortieth
2nd	second	12th	twelfth	22nd	twenty-second	50th	fiftieth
3rd	third	13th	thirteenth	23rd	twenty-third	60th	sixtieth
4th	fourth	14th	fourteenth	24th	twenty-fourth	70th	seventieth
5th	fifth	15th	fifteenth	25th	twenty-fifth	80th	eightieth
6th	sixth	16th	sixteenth	26th	twenty-sixth	90th	ninetieth
7th	seventh	17th	seventeenth	27th	twenty-seventh	100th	hundredth
8th	eighth	18th	eighteenth	28th	twenty-eighth	1,000th	thousandth
9th	ninth	19th	nineteenth	29th	twenty-ninth	1,000,000th	millionth

Days of the week

Monday
Tuesday
Wednesday
Thursday
Friday
Saturday
Sunday

Months of the year

January	July
February	August
March	September
April	October
May	November
June	December

Verb forms

Simple present

I work	I do not work	Do I work?
You work	You do not work	Do you work?
He / she works	He / she does not work	Does he / she work?
We work	We do not work	Do we work?
You work	You do not work	Do you work?
They work	They do not work	Do they work?

Present continuous

I am working	I am not working	Am I working?
You are working	You are not working	Are you working?
He / she is working	He / she is not working	Is he / she working?
We are working	We are not working	Are we working?
You are working	You are not working	Are you working?
They are working	They are not working	Are they working?

Simple past

I worked	I did not work	Did I work?
You worked	You did not work	Did you work?
He / she worked	He / she did not work	Did he / she work?
We worked	We did not work	Did we work?
You worked	You did not work	Did you work?
They worked	They did not work	Did they work?

Past continuous

I was working	I was not working	Was I working?
You were working	You were not working	Were you working?
He / she was working	He / she was not working	Was he / she working?
We were working	We were not working	Were we working?
You were working	You were not working	Were you working?
They were working	They were not working	Were they working?

Future

I shall / will work	I shall / will not work	Shall / will I work?
You will work	You will not work	Will you work?
He / she will work	He / she will not work	Will he / she work?
We shall / will work	We shall / will not work	Shall / will we work?
You will work	You will not work	Will you work?
They will work	They will not work	Will they work?

Contractions

I'm	**I am**	**I don't**	**I do not**
He's	**He is**	**He doesn't**	**He does not**
We're	**We are**	**I didn't**	**I did not**
You're	**You are**		
They're	**They are**	**I'll**	**I shall / will**
		He'll	**He will**
He isn't	**He is not**	**He won't**	**He will not**
They aren't	**They are not**		
		I can't	**I cannot**
I wasn't	**I was not**	**I mustn't**	**I must not**
You weren't	**You were not**		
I've	**I have**		
He's	**He has**		
I haven't	**I have not**		
He hasn't	**He has not**		

Word list

In general, the numbers refer to the chapters.

t

u

v

w

y

Imprimé en France — IMPRIMERIE HÉRISSEY, Évreux (Eure) - N° 55133
Dépôt légal : Juillet 1991 – N° d'édition : 0263-15